Take A Rifle From A Dead Man

By

Larry Matthews

A novel of one man's extraordinary
life based on a true story

Argus Enterprises International, Inc
New Jersey*****North Carolina

Take a Rifle From a Dead Man © 2013
All rights reserved by Larry Matthews

A-Argus Better Book Publishers, LLC
For information:
A-Argus Better Book Publishers, LLC
9001 Ridge Hill Street
Kernersville, North Carolina 27285
www.a-argusbooks.com

ISBN: 978-0-6157888-8-3
ISBN: 0-6157888-8-2

Book Cover designed by Dubya
Printed in the United States of America

This is a novel about one man's extraordinary life. It is based on real events.

Certain scenes, characters and dialogue were created by the author.

I Sang Dixie
Words and music by Dwight Yoakum

In memory of
Command Sergeant Major Lawrence. C. Matthews
United States Army

The End

He was old and he was empty. He sat shirtless and shoeless on the sofa in the living room of the house he had shared with his wife in the two decades of his retirement. They had been together since the days of their youth—through three wars, the years in Europe as a spy, and the years of his drinking and decline. Now it was over. She had gone to take a nap and that was the end. He stared at the floor and assumed that she had simply had enough of him and decided that it was time for her heart to stop. *Stop the pain. Stop the love. Stop it. Stop it.*

He was a small man now. His hair was thin and gray and wild on his head like some mad professor who had stuck his finger in a light socket. His face was sunken and he hadn't shaved in five days. In that moment he looked like a derelict on the street. Even so, he was still lean and muscular in a way that revealed a life of suffering and combat. He was a man who struggled with ghosts and the faces of those who had died at his hands. He had never meant to live that life. He was—in his heart—a poet and a scholar, a man who not only had read the classics but could recite entire passages. He was a student of history and the ancient Greeks.

He was also a recognized firearms expert, a black belt in Judo, a skilled knife fighter, and a man who knew precisely where and how to use a blackjack. He could pick virtually any lock in seconds. He could survive behind enemy lines. What he could not do was live an ordinary life, a challenge he had failed in the years since he took his retirement as a Command Sergeant Major of the United States Army.

He looked up at his son, who was at a loss to comfort the father. "We need to hug," he said in a voice that betrayed his upbringing in the hills of northern Alabama. The son moved to the sofa and the two men embraced. The old man put his hands to his face and wept.

"You don't know what it's like to take a rifle from a dead man to survive," he said.

"No," the son replied, "I don't."

The old man went to a record player and put a disk on the turntable. "I want you to hear something." The arm swung down, the needle popped onto the record and the voice of Dwight Yoakum filled the small room.

I sang Dixie, as he died
But people just walked on by, as I cried
The bottle had robbed him of all his rebel pride
So I sang Dixie, as he died

The old man cried and stared at his son. This was his song, his story, and he wanted the son to understand.

He said, "Listen to me son while you still can. Run back home to that Southern land
Don't you see what life here has done to me?"
Then he closed those old blue eyes, and fell limp, against my side
No more pain, and now he's safe back home in Dixie.

The song ended and there was only the noise of the turntable's arm returning to its resting place. The old man sat beneath the gun rack that held three rifles and a shotgun, and stared at his son.

"She's buried ten miles due north. I'm heading north to be with her. I need you to get me there. Do you follow me?"

"I can't do it," the son said. "You are dying. It won't be much longer."

"You can't let me suffer."

"I won't do this."

The old man began to cough, a racking, bloody mess that overtook him almost hourly these days. He coughed until he had no more in him and sat exhausted and pale. "Then you can take me to the VA hospital."

Four days later the old man was dead, and two days after that he was headed due north to be with the woman who had tolerated him and worried about him for forty years. After the funeral the son went back to the house and sat on the sofa. He went to the record player and watched as the needle dropped.

No more pain, and now he's safe back home in Dixie

The Beginning

The 1920's

Chapter one

"But I, being poor, have only my dreams. I have spread my dreams under your feet; tread softly, because you tread on my dreams." William Butler Yeats

The wagon came down the mountain before dawn, in the absolute darkness that electricity would banish in a little more than a decade. The spring leaves were full and offered cover against the starlight that fell that night on Jackson County, Alabama. The mule that pulled the wagon was outraged at its task and pulled from side to side as the man on the seat cursed and snapped the leather straps on the uphill sections of the journey and held the brake on the steep downhill slopes that led to the flat land and the Tennessee River.

There were three people in the wagon. The man who held the reins was red-haired, in his mid-twenties, and wore a government-issue wooden leg below his left knee, the result of his service in France in the war that had ended three years earlier. Beside him was a tiny, angry forty-one-year-old woman who cursed like a man. In the back under a blanket was a fifteen-year-old-girl who was very pregnant and screaming in pain. She was resting on a bed of hay that was wet from the day's rain.

"Damn, Momma! It hurts. How much longer?" The girl was in labor and she was frightened. She was barely taller than her mother and a diet of pokeweed and bacon drippings had left her thin and weak.

"Dammit! You done this to yourself, girl. Don't you go makin' a racket all the way." The older woman was her mother, a Chocktaw whose people had stayed behind after the great migration to Oklahoma. Her name was Sarah and aside from certain physical characteristics she was a common hillbilly. She was four feet ten, weighed just over eighty pounds, and was as mean as a snake.

"You gonna be fine, Mary." The man's name was Paul Brite and he was Mary's husband, the nuptials having recently been achieved at the end of a ten gauge shotgun.

"You bleedin'?" Sarah asked the question as a statement of anger.

"Hell, yes, I'm bleedin'."

"It's the devil's way of telling you you ain't nothin' but a whore."

And so it went at four miles to the hour all the way to South Pittsburg, across the line in Tennessee, where there was a hospital. A day later, Mary gave birth to a boy and named him after his father. The boy was born into a world of poverty and brutality that would stain his life and rip through his soul until he met his maker, seven decades later.

The 1920's weren't roaring in the mountains of the South. For most of those folks, the people whose homes were described by city-dwellers as "back up in there," life was hard and short. Children died of disease and lack of nutrition, mothers died in childbirth, and men died of gunshots, knife wounds, or accidents. It was a time of yellow fever, malaria, hookworm, and pellagra.

The Great Depression was still over the horizon for much of the country but for the rural South it was already a reality. Overworked land had cut farm yields and the boll weevil cut the cotton crop to pieces. The people on the farms and in the hills had bad health and no money. They lived in shacks that had no electricity, plumbing, or hope. They ate what they could grow, find, or kill. The smart ones got out and went to Chattanooga, where electricity was changing the way the world worked. It wasn't perfect but it was better than starving to death in the dark.

Mary Brite, young Paul's pretty mother, had no use for the old ways. "I ain't spending my days eating poke and crappin' babies," she said. "I got me some ideas about life and they ain't here on this farm." As she said it, she was the picture of the Hillbilly Madonna, wearing a flour sack dress and holding a squalling infant to her adolescent breast.

"You got that damn brat now, so you done made your bed, you and him." Sarah pointed to Paul Senior, who was taking a pull of moonshine out of a jar. "He ain't no better'n your daddy. He'll leave you to starve while he goes after his pleasure." Sarah's late husband Joseph had been a cold man of no particular feeling who had once grabbed his things and gone fishing while the house was on fire, leaving his wife and children to form a bucket line to save what they could.

"Paul and me, we got plans to be fancy in Chattanooga; ain't that right, Paul."

Paul looked up, unfocused, and nodded. It was plain to Sarah that whatever ambition was in the air was being breathed by Mary.

It was a time of change in America and Mary could smell it from the inside of a cabin where life was as it had been for centuries. Within its interior, light was offered by coal oil and food was cooked on an iron stove. The scent of human bodies was overpowering and endless nights were spent waiting for the dawn and fresh air. There was no elegance and there was no comfort, only the daily struggle to survive and the acceptance of disease and death as companions on the road to eternity.

A wagon trip of a few hours could bring a person across time to a new world of artificial light that offered magic and gaiety and a feeling that life was worth living. A new Ford automobile cost less than three hundred dollars. People in the city could work and make enough money to buy a car and a new suit of clothes. A person could walk into a café and order bacon and eggs and have it brought right to the table. Mary had no plans to stay where she was. She would do whatever it took.

Mary and Paul Sr. lit out for the city, leaving Paul Jr. with Sarah in the mean shack back up in there. Chattanooga might as well have been Paris for Mary. There was electricity, cars, even radio. Women wore short hair and even shorter skirts. Men wore suits and snappy hats. The air was filled with the scent of perfume, hair oil, and auto exhaust. There was music in the clubs that offered the high octane booze that was produced in great quantities in the nearby hills, Prohibition be damned.

Mary wasn't the most sophisticated teenage girl in the world but she knew the power of what she had and she was unburdened by religious belief or quaint notions of morality. Paul was also unburdened by such things and was happy to enjoy the benefits of a wife who knew how to pry money out of other men's wallets. He was content to drink and play pool, shoot craps and flirt with women who would lift their skirts for a dollar, and wait for his young wife to flash a little cash.

Back on the farm Paul Jr. was learning to walk and talk. Sarah was a somber presence in his life and she rarely smiled. But she had one gift that could offer what would be a lifelong joy to the boy. Sarah could read. As a girl, she had spent four years in a country schoolhouse learning the basic subjects of arithmetic, English, and the history of the South. The reading had led her to books that took her away from the misery of her life. Paul Jr. sat on her lap every evening and stared at her face as she read to him, not knowing what the stories were about, but taken by the magic in her voice. He was eighteen months old when he first was exposed to the words of Nathaniel Hawthorne. He could read on his own before his fifth birthday.

Mary and Paul Sr. had another child, a girl, two years later when Mary was seventeen, and then she sent Paul Sr. packing. He would be replaced by a long line of men of uncertain temperament and criminal intent. Mary would never be described as a moral woman but she put in her time on occasion to show her face to her children.

Chapter two

Mary was a sociopath in that she had very little feeling for others, even her own children. She believed that she had only one thing to trade for a better life and she set out to learn its value. The men who passed through her bed were rough, stupid, smart, clean, dirty, clever and dense. Some stayed for days, some for months. In the end, she got more than she gave and she learned how to read men and find their weaknesses. She was tiny and seductive and men wanted to take care of her and make her their own. Some of them taught the finer points of "the life."

The 1920's were prime years for con artists. People coming to the cities from the countryside were willing to believe anything if strong hooch and a hint of sex were involved. City folks were willing to believe they were too smart to be conned and so were easy marks for smooth talkers with a story to tell. "Everybody's a mark," one of her men said. "Ain't nothin' wrong with getting' what they got."

Mary became an expert at two cons: the Spanish Prisoner and the Badger. The Spanish Prisoner was a con in which the mark was told some cash had been found and once the hook had been set the mark would be told he would get some of it but he would first be required to put up some "good faith" money. There were many variations on the con but the key elements were greed and lust. Mary knew how to short circuit the marks' good sense, if they had any.

The Badger con is an ancient and effective form of blackmail in which a married man is placed in a compromising position and threatened with exposure if he doesn't pay up. The success of the con was not finding marks. There were plenty of those. It was finding marks that had enough ready cash to make the con worthwhile. In Chattanooga in the twenties there were more Badger players than suitable marks, so Mary learned to rise above the competition. Still, it was not an easy life but it was better than the alternative.

Down on the farm, Sarah, Paul, his little sister Elizabeth, and Sarah's eleven-year-old son Charlie were surviving on poke—which grew wild—water cress from the pond, and corn meal, which was as precious as cash. Sarah, as tough as ever, managed to hold things together and harangued her daughter into sending a little money now and then.

Charlie was a wild child, an unfocused boy who spent his days being a burden to those around him. If he did his chores he did them poorly. He snuck sips of the moonshine Sarah kept for "medical" purposes. He spied on the females and displayed his privates. He was a boy who was consumed with his own appetites and pleasures. Charlie was a taker, not a giver. Even so, Paul saw Charlie as a hero.

By Christmas of 1929 the four of them were desperate. Presents were out of the question. Paul took a hatchet into the woods and cut down a small pine tree and dragged it to the cabin, where he propped it in a corner. Sarah and Elizabeth took fabric scraps left from a quilt and placed them on the tree. Sarah went to a small box, removed the remaining change and took the wagon to a general store where she purchased a box of .22 shells. The clerk gave her a small square of colored paper and she wrapped the shells and placed them under the tree on Christmas morning.

After a breakfast of corn meal and lard, Sarah handed the box to Paul. "Here's Christmas," she said, without joy.

The boy felt the weight of the box and knew what it was. He was only eight years old but he could pick a squirrel out of a tree with the single-shot rifle that was kept by the door. He opened the box as his sister and grandmother looked on without smiles or anticipation.

Sarah placed her hand on his head. "Now you need to go get us something for dinner," she said. "Don't waste any of these. We may need them to get through the winter."

The boy took six shells from the box and placed them in his shirt pocket. He went to the door, put on an old coat that was several sizes too big, picked up the rifle and went out into the morning air, listening to the sound of his steps on the frost that covered the wild gamma grass in the field near the cabin. He loaded a shell and walked to the tree line and waited. An hour later the boy returned to the cabin with a rabbit and five shells. His natural skill with a firearm would serve him well throughout his life.

Mary came home to the farm on occasion to hide from one problem or another; sometimes a sheriff, sometimes a swindled man. She had developed the habit of marrying the men she lived with and casually tossing them aside when she was no longer interested. Tennessee courts saw her as just another immoral hillbilly and granted her divorces as a matter of course, holding her to a lower standard than, say, a doctor's wife. These "husbands" were brought along on her trips to the farm and they were a low-rent parade of Southern bottom feeders, given to high-waisted pleated trousers, fedoras, and thin mustaches known as "pussy bumpers" in the popular phrase of the day.

These men were rounders, drunks, thieves, swindlers and layabouts, who were every mother's nightmare. Mary liked them because they were unburdened by the decency that kept most people out of the pockets of strangers.

One of these men went by the name of Jubal Early Atkins. His father had served with the Confederate general of the same name and felt he owed it to the general to pass it along to the boy, who was born some twenty years after the War. Young Jubal was, like Charlie Brite, an unfocused natural born rounder who had the good fortune to be the possessor of perfect teeth, something that was rare in a time of poor nutrition and even poorer hygiene. Jubal's smile was dazzling under his straight black hair and deep blue eyes. He could, and had, charmed the pants off the ladies.

Sarah saw him for what he was and refused to speak to him or even offer him food, which was in short supply anyway. Jubal took offense and spent his days brooding and feeling sorry for himself, sinking into an ugly anger as he sipped from the moonshine jar.

"You people need to respect me," he said. "I ain't some lowlife you can treat bad." Jubal was vain about his hair and kept it well oiled and plastered against his head in a style he believed made him look like Rudolph Valentino, the star of silent action films and the fantasy of women from coast to coast. Jubal was vain but not fastidious and his greasy hair was flecked with dandruff and stuck out at odd angles where he had slept on it.

Paul was fascinated by him and sat staring the man, wondering how he managed to shave his mustache into such a small line. The boy was careful not to sit too close because of the smell of rancid hair oil and body odor that Jubal expelled. The strong odor of boozy breath added to the unpleasantness of the man, but to Paul he was a creature to be studied, like a wild animal.

"What the hell are you lookin' at, you dang brat?" Jubal's face was a sneer.

"Nothin'."

"You callin' me nothin', boy?"

"I ain't sayin' nothin'. Just lookin' is all."

Jubal jumped up and grabbed Paul, picking him up and carrying him out the door. "Me and him is havin' a little talk. We'll be right back. Ain't nothin' to worry about so y'all stay right here." The others were silent and watched through the window as Jubal carried Paul into the small barn where the mule was kept.

Jubal was not a strong man and was soft by the standards of the rural South, but he had no trouble overpowering an eight-year-old boy. He carried Paul over his shoulder and dropped him near the stall where the mule was chewing some field grass. The stall was marked by tree trunks that had been shaved of their bark and placed upright to support the roof of the barn. A few branches that were little more than sticks were stacked horizontally to separate the stall from the rest of the barn. Leather straps and harnesses were hanging from hooks or dangling from the dividing branches.

Jubal set the boy down and pressed his face against the post that was closest to the mule. "I'm gonna teach you who to look at, boy." The man grabbed a leather strap and used it to tie the boy to the post. "I'm your daddy now and it's time you learned some manners." He removed his belt and stepped back. Jubal swung the belt at the boy's back. He kept at it for nearly an hour, tearing the shirt off the boy and creating first red whelps, then shallow cuts, then bloody gashes. Paul screamed and cried for Jubal to stop, but screams only sent Jubal into a deeper fury.

Jubal began to dance and scream insults at the boy, telling him he was worthless and that his mother was no good whore. He whipped the bloody belt over his head and alternated his attack between the boy and the mule. His face was red and he was dripping greasy sweat onto the dirt floor. The mule began to dance and rear up against the noise and the belt. The man ignored the common sense rule against standing behind an agitated mule. The animal kicked back, connecting with Jubal's hip bone, propelling the hollering man through the opposite side of the barn, where old boards were held in place by rusty nails.

Sarah, Mary and Charlie ran out of the house and found Jubal nearly unconscious and unable to move, Paul tied and bloody, and the mule about to pull down the barn. Sarah went back into the house and grabbed the rifle, loaded it, and walked to where Jubal lay in the ground. She lifted the rifle and aimed at Jubal's privates.

Mary stepped in front of her mother. "Don't you shoot him. He's my husband."

Sarah looked at her daughter. "Quite a man you got there, ain't he? Beats up a boy like that. I wish that mule had killed him."

"Paul had it comin'. He can't go around looking at people like that."

"He ain't had it comin'. You better get that no account outta here or I will shoot him and not think a thing of it."

Mary and Jubal had arrived at the farm in a used Durant automobile that the couple had swindled from a mark in Chattanooga. Mary and Charlie managed to get Jubal onto the back seat and she drove away, shouting curses at her mother. Jubal's broken hip led to complications and he died in pain one month later.

Paul bore the scars of the whipping until the day he died.

The 1930's

Chapter three

Get on. Ride hard. Hold nothing back, and give it all you've got! That's the Cowboy Way!!!
Western Proverb

The great stock market crash up in New York did not mean anything to the four people who lived in Sarah's cabin. Life did not change for them or for anyone they knew in the hills of northern Alabama and Tennessee. Life was hard before the crash and it was hard after. The Chattanooga newspapers were full of stories about stock brokers jumping out of windows and people in soup lines in the northern cities. For Sarah and Charlie, Paul and Elizabeth, soup was a luxury. Had any do-gooders turned up outside their door with a pot of nutritious soup, they would have been grateful for the miracle. As it was, they were thankful that poke grew in the fields and watercress in the pond. They spent their evenings by the light of coal oil lamps and allowed themselves the dream of something better.

Paul and Elizabeth attended a community school that served children like themselves and learned the arithmetic, reading, English, penmanship, history, and basic science. Paul was smart and eager to learn and he consumed books with a hunger that matched his desire for a decent meal. For Paul's tenth birthday Charlie produced a cigar he had cadged from the owner of the general store with a lie about getting good grades in school. Charlie was not a scholar. His talent was his way with words and a smile, especially with the older girls, who allowed him liberties.

Paul and Charlie smoked the cigar in the woods near the house and dreamed of what was over the hill.

"You ever think about getting' outta here?" Charlie asked.

"Ever' day," Paul said. "I'm gonna get gone when I can."

"We can leave together," Charlie said. He choked on the cigar smoke and went into a coughing fit." I'll show you what's happenin' out yonder and away from here."

The boys made a secret pact to light out someday.

Charlie ran off a year later, just after his fourteenth birthday, and moved in with his sister in Chattanooga. Mary was not an attentive young woman but she was willing to teach Charlie some of the tricks to surviving on the weakness of others. He learned to cheat at cards but the men he tried to cheat were on to the game and he suffered a few beatings. And he learned act the pimp in a version of the Murphy game, in this case blackmailing or robbing gullible men who thought they were going to have sex with Mary. Most of the marks were poor, given the state of things, but a dollar here and a dollar there would keep them both in cornbread. Mary was between husbands at the time.

Paul remained on the farm and grew into a thin, handsome teenager who could recite poetry and write for the local weekly newspaper, two skills that were lacking in nearly every other young man in the region. He won cash or food in shooting contests. Like his Uncle Charlie, he could talk the girls out of their bloomers.

Sarah saw him as a wild child and felt it necessary to smack him down on occasion and ordered him to stand still while she climbed up on a chair to slap his face. He was a foot taller and she liked to look him in the eye as she smacked him. "Ain't nothin' in life easy, boy. Whatever you get you get yourself. You remember that."

Paul saw the farm as a small and hard boiled world ruled by a desperate and angry woman. Sarah spent her days in serious concern about the day to follow and saw every bite of food as a prize to be fought over. She never missed a chance to tell him his mother was a no good whore and Charlie was no better than a low down snake. "You can do better, boy. You don't need to lie down with Satan to get through your life. Learn to use your brain and you won't have to make a livin' with your body." In those moments she was capable of expressing an unspeakable sadness.

His mother was a sometimes presence in his life, a woman who wore fancy city dresses and thick perfume. Even so, she smelled like tobacco and alcohol. She smiled at her men and laughed at her mother. She paraded husbands around the family and never spoke of them again.

Charlie had the arrogance of a young grifter and a smile that said he saw most other people as marks. "Life is a good time," was his personal motto, which he shared with everyone, marks and friends alike. He brought cigars, moonshine, and sexy photographs to the farm and shared them with Paul, who spent his nights dreaming of the women in the pictures and life on the road away from northern Alabama.

Charlie had ridden the rails, catching out, as it was known, on the freight cars that were filling up with the detritus of America, and he had stories to tell of other places where people sang and played guitars, rode horses over the prairies, and spent their time with willing girls who would do anything for a charming Southern boy. Charlie had learned to tell his stories with a toothpick in his mouth, a habit he thought made him appear to be dashing and experienced in the ways of the world. For Paul, just past his fourteenth birthday, it was time to hit the road.

By 1935 the people of the mountain South were as low as they had ever been. Hard times were part of life in good times and the thirties were hardly good for anyone. The Depression sent hundreds of thousands of people from all over the country off in search of survival. There were no jobs. There was no money. Families couldn't feed their children. Schools closed. Farms were abandoned. Children roamed America in search of whatever they could find.

Sarah was beside herself with worry and responsibility for Paul and Elizabeth. The simple fact was there was not enough to eat and no way to get what they needed. Even the rabbits were in short supply. They'd been mostly hunted down by desperate people looking for something to put on the table.

Paul was a growing boy and he was hungry most of the time. He consoled himself with his books but words were no substitute for protein. Charlie made a visit, driving a car whose ownership was uncertain, and pulled Paul aside.

"Let's you and me catch out and go have some fun," he said.

"What's that mean," Paul asked.

"Catch out. Ride the rails. We'll find a hobo jungle and hit the road. What the hell, let's do it."

Millions of Americans were riding the rails in the mid-thirties. The Southern Pacific alone reported over a half million people had been thrown off its freight trains in 1932. A man named C.C. Carstens ran the Child Welfare League of America and told a Congressional committee that the number of children wandering America in those years might be as high as one million.

Paul and Charlie joined them by way of the Nashville, Chattanooga and St. Louis railroad. Never again would Paul eat pokeweed or pour old bacon grease over watercress for dinner.

Chapter four

The freight yards in Chattanooga were the engine that powered whatever commerce was left in Southern Appalachia in those years. The city called itself "The dynamo of Dixie," a term that rang a bit hollow during the Depression, when the dynamo had run out of steam. *Chattanooga Choochoo*, the song that would make the city's passenger terminal famous, was years away.

Four terminals served passengers and freight when Paul and Charlie stepped over the tracks to a hobo jungle set up near a creek in a grove of trees near the freight lines. It was nearly dark on a warm evening and two dozen or so people were flopped on the ground, staring at a fire in a cut-off barrel. Two forked sticks had been stuck in the dirt next to the barrel and an iron pot was suspended over the fire.

An older man whose face was dirty and needed a shave tended the pot and turned to watch Paul and Charlie approach the jungle. "You boys got anything for the pot? You ain't jungle buzzards, are ya?" A jungle buzzard was a man who hung around hobo camps looking for free food and liquor.

"We got some hooch if that'll get us a meal," Charlie said, sitting down next to a girl who wore a boy's haircut. "How you doin', darlin'?" He smiled at the girl, who turned away.

The man stepped away from the fire and pushed his hat back on his head. "How much hooch?"

"How much meal?"

"You'll get your share. Gimme a looksee."

Charlie carried a bed roll tied with string and he pulled it off his shoulder, inserted a hand into the roll, and produced a Mason jar filled with clear liquid. "Smooth as water and it'll kick your ass."

"Can't say the same about this grub but it'll sure taste better goin' down after that hooch." The older man stared at the jar and Charlie knew he was measuring his chance of taking it away from the two boys.

Paul had seen hard men all his life, men whose bodies were strong and whose spirits were cold. This man was hard and Paul sensed that he ruled the jungle. Paul wanted to leave. "Maybe we need to find somewhere else to light," he said, nudging Charlie.

The man stepped forward and smiled at the boys. "They call me Hatchet. What're you two known as?" He leaned back with the look of a man about to eat a puppy.

Charlie put the Mason jar back into the bed roll and backed away. "They call me Chattanooga Charlie and this here's Tennessee Slim." He jerked his thumb in Paul's direction. Paul had never heard his hobo nickname before.

"I've been ridin' the rails for quite a spell and I never heard of you boys," Hatchet said. "You new around here?" He jumped forward and grabbed Charlie by the back of his neck. "I asked you a question, boy."

"Listen, mister, we'll just keep movin'. We didn't mean nothin' by comin' in here." Charlie's voice was thin and hysterical.

"Then you better just leave that hooch with me before you move along. I'm goin' north and east tonight and I don't want to see you boys movin' my way. You got that? You two Angelinas are gonna need to grow some big ones if you're gonna beat your way around. There's some tough sons of bitches on these rails." Angelina was a term used to describe a young kid on the road.

Charlie gave the Mason jar to Hatchet and he and Paul walked up to the rail yard where freight cars were being connected into the trains that would move to all points of the compass that night. The yard smelled like coal dust and rotting produce and Paul wondered if he had found a new version of Hell. It was a flat yard and locomotives were used to assemble the trains. Other yards were called hump yards and gravity was used to move cars down shallow inclines. The rail yard workmen hollered and blew whistles, the locomotives chugged and spewed thick smoke, and the cars banged together in loud clanks and screeches.

Railroad bulls hired to keep rail riders off the trains roamed the yard with four-foot clubs, looking for hobos and tramps sneaking onto freight cars. The bulls no longer bothered to call the police when they found the riders. There were too many of them. They now beat the trespassers with the clubs and sent them on their way, often with missing teeth or broken bones. Even so, by the time the freight trains reached the outskirts of Chattanooga they were carrying as many men and women, boys and girls, as the cars could hold. Some would stumble and die under the trains. Others would get into fights on the trains and be thrown to their deaths. Some were there for adventure, others were on the run. But a great majority was on the trains to survive the Depression.

As a warm dawn rose over the mountains, a long freight train picked up steam as it left the yard, carrying pine logs from Georgia, early produce from Alabama, and pigs from Southern farms. The train was headed west, to Nashville, Memphis, through Arkansas, and, eventually, to south Texas, where it would be reassembled in San Antonio and carry produce back east. Aboard a boxcar loaded with walnuts and other Southern products, Paul and Charlie looked out between the slats at the passing city and then the greenery of the fields and forests. Paul felt a moment of pure elation. He had never felt so free and so happy. "Whoowee!" he shouted.

"Pipe down, goddam it!" came a voice from behind the boxes. "People are sleeping here."

"Not me!" Paul shouted back. "I'm on my own."

Chapter five

Paul's mother Mary had brought occasional joy into the boy's life by taking him to the city and showing him the sights. These rare trips to her world were always marked by an afternoon at the movies, where westerns thrilled kids who had never seen the West or a cowboy. Paul's favorite movie star was Tom Mix, who rode a horse named Tony. Tom Mix was "King of the Cowboys" long before Roy Rodgers claimed the title. He set the standard for cowboy movie stars and boys like Paul assumed he had been born in Texas, grew up on a ranch, and spent his life fighting Indians and bad guys.

In truth, he was born and grew up in Pennsylvania where his father was stable master for a wealthy lumber magnate. His father taught him to ride. He joined the army during the Spanish American War, went AWOL and never returned to his unit. He was never court martialed or even discharged and he managed to ride in Teddy Roosevelt's inaugural parade, prompting later Hollywood publicists to mistakenly claim he had been a Rough Rider.

Through showmanship and horsemanship, Tom Mix was every boy's hero in the early thirties and Paul had spent many hungry nights seeking sleep and dreaming of riding the West on Tony, "The Wonder Horse." The man and the horse appeared together in nearly two-hundred movies. Tony even appeared in movies by himself, doing spectacular stunts.

Paul stood atop a freight car as it left Dallas and gazed out upon the flat Texas landscape and allowed himself a moment of joy. He was in Texas and he was young and wild. The train made its way south, across small, shallow rivers and through towns that had buildings confined to one side of the street. People in the towns lined up to watch the train come through. Some towns had handmade signs warning the hobos not to get off the train. "We don't have jobs for our own so we don't want you here," they said.

Most of the roads were dirt and some were nothing more than wide paths. Movement on the roads was often a buckboard pulled by a team. Model A pickups were spotted here and there, but not many. Times were tough and pickups cost money. Houses were few and far apart. Horses and cattle dotted the landscape.

It was all magic for Paul. The rail riders lounged on top of the freight cars and let America roll by beneath them. They were hungry and desperate, but most of them were young and felt the excitement of a child on Christmas morning when all things were possible and all dreams could come true.

Ranch work is not what it appears to be in the movies. It is hard, dirty work that never ends. There is rarely the singing of cowboy songs by the fire while a pretty girl looks on in admiration. It's work that even desperate men avoid when they can. To boys like Paul it was living the life of Tom Mix, despite the low pay and long hours. Paul and Charlie found jobs on a dusty ranch fifty miles southwest of San Antonio, known to the tramps as "San Atone."

The ranch was owned by a New Yorker who had never seen it. He was satisfied to tell his friends that he owned a Texas ranch where he raised cattle, assuming that such a property and endeavor provided a certain cache among his society friends, whose land holdings were confined to townhouses in the city and mansions in Newport.

The ranch was managed by a native Texan named Leander Johnson, a bow-legged scrapper who, as a sergeant in the army, had come to believe that the only way to manage men is to beat them into submission. There were any number of ways to accomplish this, in his opinion, and fisticuffs was only one of them. Another was hard, brutal work. For this reason, there were always job openings at the ranch as it became clear to those he hired that life there as a cowboy was worse than whatever lay beyond the horizon, however difficult that might be.

Johnson paid his cowboys twenty-dollars a month, plus a bed, plenty of beef and beans, and a horse to ride. Every one of these things was more than Paul had ever had in his life. He had never held a twenty dollar coin, had never had enough to eat, and he only ridden horses lent to him by kind people. He was not a skilled rider but he had enough experience to control a horse and not let it run off with him.

The bunkhouse where Leander Johnson's cowboys lived was a large room with army cots along the walls and a Franklin stove in the middle to provide heat in the winter. Nails were driven into the wooden walls over the cots where the cowboys could hang their clothes. Small wooden shelves had been installed near the cots and the cowboys kept water bowls for shaving, mugs for coffee, and personal items, which were few. A fancy red bandana was considered extravagant and a sign that its owner considered himself a "dandy."

The cowboys were required to wash their sheets twice a month. They were required to bath once a week, either in the stock tank—a pond where the cattle drank and shit—or under a shower at the ranch's elevated water tank, which was filled by a windmill. All of the current crop of cowboys chose the shower, even though the water was cold most of the time.

Leander Johnson believed that hard work required good food and he had a small staff of Mexicans who cooked for the cowboys. Fancy men from up north were shocked by the heat the Mexicans cooked into the beans. Some of them quit rather than eat the spicy, pepper-enhanced chow that fueled the men morning and evening. The only way to tell breakfast from dinner was the biscuits. If they were on the table, it was breakfast. Every meal was beef and beans. And cool water to wash it all down. Johnson felt that anything more would be a waste.

The men complained nonstop about the food and the work. Nights in the bunkhouse were hours of complaining and playing cards for the next month's pay. Some men had lost more than a year's wages in bets that no one expected to be paid. Alcohol was forbidden and Johnson would fire anyone who possessed it or reeked of it. Racy pictures were also forbidden as was any sex act, even those involving only one man. Hard work, no booze, no sex, beef and beans. Life on the ranch.

Paul didn't listen to the complaints. He ate the beef and beans with gratitude and he looked forward to riding the range and he secretly practiced singing a few cowboys songs from Tim Mix movies, planning to sing and yodel as he drove the cattle, "punching cattle," as the men called it.

Every group, no matter how difficult or unpleasant, has at least one man who has been there longer than anyone could reasonably expect. On this ranch that man was known as Amarillo Slim, who had worked for Leander Johnson for nearly twenty years, starting when he was a teenage orphan with no place to go. Amarillo Slim got his name as a joke when an older man made fun of him and called him the name of a gunfighter long dead. It stuck and he grew into it. By the mid-thirties he was six feet tall and weighed one-hundred-thirty-five pounds. He never smiled. His face was brown and set with deep lines. He wore a straw cowboy hat that was falling apart and filthy. He had the air of a man who could cut you down and not think a thing of it.

Johnson had Paul and Charlie doing odd jobs for two days; fixing fences, cleaning stalls, moving piles of manure, and making repairs to the bunk house. On the morning of the third day, after breakfast and as the sun was coming up, he called them over and introduced them to Amarillo Slim, who looked at the boys with an expression that said he would rather be looking at the walls of a barn.

"Boys, time for you get to work and earn your keep. Amarillo Slim here is going to introduce you to your mounts and teach you how to fix a windmill. This ranch needs water. You may have noticed that it doesn't rain much around here. We get our water from the ground. The windmills bring it up. They need upkeep. That's where you come in." He nodded at Amarillo Slim and walked away. Amarillo Slim looked at the boys and walked into a coral where a dozen horses were kept."

"Take your pick," he growled in a matter-of-fact voice that said he didn't care which ones they chose or whether they chose any at all.

One of the horses had white sox that to Paul looked just like the legs of Tony the Wonder Horse. "That one," he said, pointing. Charlie chose a spotted, sway-backed mare that Amarillo Slim dismissed as "dog meat." Half an hour later the three of them were trotting down a dirt path, past cattle grazing on what to Paul looked like scrub grass.

Paul was a natural rider and the horse was a gelding of easy nature. He could not stop smiling. "I'm gonna call him Tony," he said, "after Tom Mix's horse."

"Call him whatever you like," Amarillo Slim said. "He don't care."

"I'm just gonna call this one horse," Charlie said in a voice that revealed his distaste for whatever work was in store.

Chapter six

Fixing windmills on a Texas ranch in summer heat was as bad a job as there was in those years. As a fourteen-year-old boy on his own Paul had no way of knowing that as he rode Tony up to a wooden tower a good distance from the bunkhouse. Windmills had brought water up from the ground for centuries. By the mid-thirties a farmer or rancher could order a windmill kit from companies in the East and use hired men to assemble it into a functioning water pump. In dry areas, where rain was rare, windmills were the difference between success and failure in the cattle business.

Most of the windmills on the ranch used a wooden tower to support the pipes and mechanics that brought up the water. Windmills have many parts and they break down or jam. It can be hard and dirty work. The turbine that captures the wind has many blades that turn and adjust to wind speed. The gearbox at the top controls a crankshaft that provides reciprocating strokes to the drop pipe and pump rod that pull up the water. The pipes are inserted into the water table through a well dug by augers, a kind of large screw. The water spills into a holding container or a small pond.

High winds, heavy dust, or a long list of other causes can jam the windmill and cause it to stop pumping. On a large ranch there is always at least one of them down and in need of repair. Paul and Charlie were in for a long day. Two of the blades were broken and needed to be replaced. A bird had managed to get into the gearbox and was very dead and very jammed into the mechanism. A support slat on the tower was falling off and needed to be reattached. All of the work required Paul and Charlie to climb the tower. This one was roughly forty feet high. Paul was afraid of heights and he began to shake as Amarillo Slim worked his way up the support boards.

"C'mon, boys. C'mon up. Don't look down if your sceered. We got work needs to be done."

It took Paul fifteen minutes to climb the tower. He tried not to look down but each time he reached a new level he couldn't help himself and he glanced at the ground, which seemed very far away. He hugged the support boards and the beams that held up the tower, and he shook and worried that he would either throw up or piss his pants.

Charlie did throw up halfway to the top and needed a few minutes to get himself together before he joined Paul and Amarillo Slim at the gearbox, where the boys learned how to open the box, dig out the dead bird, and reset the gears. Replacing the blade was more difficult because it required them to extend out from the tower. Amarillo Slim got the water flowing again by mid-day and allowed the boys to soak their heads and drink their fill before they mounted up for the next job. By evening Paul was in a daze and sick to his stomach. He ate very little at dinner and spent the night in dreams of falling from high places.

Amarillo Slim spent the week teaching the boys how windmills work and how to fix them. He allowed them to work on their own on a few small jobs and checked their work to make sure the water was flowing after they had finished. Life for the boys had a routine, however unpleasant it might have seemed to them.

Paul and Charlie received their first pay one month after they arrived at the ranch. It was customary to pay young cowboys, those considered too foolish to know how to spend money, in silver dollars. The idea was that twenty silver dollars would be too heavy and bulky to carry around, prompting the cowboy to leave some of his pay behind and not spend it on payday.

Paul had never even seen twenty dollars at once and so spent the day gazing in wonder at his stack of coins. The cowboys were allowed to leave the ranch to visit a cantina that was located on the outskirts of the nearest town, a dusty village called Arroyo Benito. The town was dry, meaning alcohol sales were forbidden. The end of Prohibition in 1933 did not impress the local grandees, who remembered the days of drunken cowboys and all that they brought with them. Not that these grandees themselves were dry. They preferred to drink in the privacy of their homes with those they chose.

One concession to the need of the local ranch workers to let off steam was the cantina, kept away from the town's stores and ranch supply businesses. It had no name and didn't need one. Cantina was enough of a name for those who spent their wages there. The last week of the month was slow and the clientele were mostly drifters and hobos hoping to cadge a free drink and sandwich. The first week of the month, when the cowboys were flush, was very busy and brought in women of a certain morality who were willing to offer the services that the men had spent the past month dreaming about. Violence was not unknown during the monthly spells, mostly over women and cards.

Working cowboys in the thirties carried handguns, rifles, and shotguns as a matter of routine. Coyotes, snakes and injured cattle needed to be dealt with. There was very little gun violence, except during pay week, when a bottle of tequila could alter a man's good sense. Firearms were forbidden in the cantina, but didn't mean they weren't carried. Experienced hands said they carried handguns because others did. The ban was enforced but not effectively.

The ranch where Paul and Charlie worked provided a flatbed truck to carry the men to the cantina on Saturday nights following payday, always the first day of the month. The men climbed aboard and sat where they could for the trip, which took less than an hour. There were no slats on the sides of the truck bed, so some of the men let their legs hang off and stared out at the passing landscape as the sun set.

Paul and Charlie stood on the truck bed near the cab and smiled at each other. The cantina was, to all practical purposes, an illegal establishment, although no law officer had ever attempted to close it or even drop by to see what was happening, other than an investigation into an occasional shooting or knife incident. Therefore, no one would ask either boy how old they were or whether they were allowed to drink. Possession of the price of a drink was all the identification that was needed. Paul had five silver dollars in his pocket. Charlie had eight.

The place would never be described as elegant. Or even decent. It was something out of the Wild West to Paul's eyes. The building was a low structure with a flat roof supported by wooden posts that were nothing more than tree trunks stripped of their bark. Sheets of tin had been nailed to the posts to form walls. There was no sign or any other indicator of the establishment. To the left was a series of hitching posts where a half dozen horses were tied. Near them was a wooden stock tank fed by a small windmill. A young cowboy was watering his horse and eying the front door of the cantina, an opening covered by a section of canvas that was tattered and filthy at the bottom, where it dragged over the dirt.

To the right was a dirt parking area where a few trucks were stopped at odd angles as ranch hands climbed down with smiles on their faces and dollars in their pockets. There was whooping and hollering and some back slapping as the men walked in.

The place was dark. The illumination, such as it was, came from coal oil lamps that were nailed to the support beams that held up the roof. The floor was dirt and uneven in the dance area where many boots on the feet of drunken men had stomped and scraped to the music of a small Mexican band made up of Vaqueros who constituted a separate class of ranch worker in Texas. They were paid less, treated poorly, and fired first.

To the right was pool table that was reasonably level, given the floor, and over it were suspended two lamps with reflectors to direct the light downward so the players could see what they were doing. A small group of men stood around the table holding mugs of beer and watching two men play eight ball.

A bar was set up along the back wall where two angry-looking men served liquor and beer to the new arrivals. The bartenders were under orders to raise prices by a nickel a glass for every round and to add another nickel a glass every hour. The price of a beer would double by midnight and hard liquor would go to a dollar a shot, an unheard of price in that part of Texas.

Five women were sitting at the bar. All of them looked sad and worn out. They were facing an evening of meeting the physical needs of men who had neither social skills nor a basic understanding of personal hygiene. Some of them had showered or taken a dip in a stock tank to wash off the dust and sweat, but most of them were as ripe as the melons that rotted outside. As with the booze, the price went up as the evening progressed. When the last cowboy went out the door the women would hand their earnings to the owner of the cantina, who would count the money and take half.

Paul and Charlie walked into the cantina with the joy that only teenagers who see their fantasies coming true can experience. Charlie was an old hand, or so he said, and led Paul to the bar and ordered two beers.

"Two bits apiece," said the bartender. "You boys ever do this before?"

"Hell yes," said Charlie, standing tall and leaning back on his boot heels.

Paul just stared at the bartender, then at his mug of beer. He had been around moonshine all his life but had never tasted alcohol. He picked up the mug and blew the foam off the liquid, mimicking the other men. He tilted the mug to his lips and took a sip. It was awful. It was bitter and tasted something like urine to him. He wondered if someone was playing a joke on him. He saw Charlie downing half of his beer in one gulp and other men enjoying the liquid in their mugs, so he took another sip, and another. He forced it down until the mug was empty, then he ordered another. He was soon tipsy and smiling at Charlie, the bartender, and any cowboy who walked by.

One of the women, an older gringo with ratty hair and too much makeup, walked up to him and grabbed his crotch. "Lookin' for a good time?" Paul thought she was the ugliest woman he had ever seen. Fifteen minutes later he was out of money and trying to remember what it felt like to be with her. He managed to get back to the truck where he fell asleep.

The drunker Charlie became the luckier he felt. He avoided the ladies and went to the pool table to watch the action there. The cowboys who were playing were even drunker and missed most of their shots, to the whoops and shouts of the onlookers, who were also drunk. Charlie signaled that he wanted a game and got a cue stick after watching for half an hour or so. He went through a ritual of checking the stick to see if it was straight, which it wasn't, and he chalked the tip with a grand gesture of showmanship, drawing some hoots from the other men. A coin was tossed and Charlie won the break.

He broke the rack with a bang and watched as the balls spread over the table. Nothing dropped. "A dollar a ball?" He gave his opponent a smile.

"Ain't gonna happen, friend," the man said. "Dime a ball. Take it or leave it." The man seemed to sober up as he picked his shot. They were playing eight ball and the man sank three stripes before Charlie got his chance.

Charlie's bad character took over. He decided to cheat. He sank two easy shots and moved two of his solid color balls to spots closer to the pockets as he maneuvered around the table to place his shots. He was clumsy and he was playing with an experienced shark who was himself trying to cheat. Charlie's opponent was better at it and had seen moves Charlie couldn't imagine. The man had no trouble spotting Charlie's moves. He was quick to anger. He waited until Charlie leaned over the table to shoot, then grabbed his cue by the small end and used it as a club on Charlie's back, knocking him to the table.

The other men crowded around, waiting for Charlie to use his own cue. The drunken cowboys were hoping to see a bloody fight. What they saw instead was a beating. Charlie was stunned and unable to respond as the other man clubbed him. He was left bleeding on the table, his scalp ripped open, two ribs cracked, and one of his legs with a hairline fracture that would take time to heal.

When it was over, the man went through Charlie's pockets and removed the silver dollars that were left. He showed them to the other men and said, "Fair and square." They murmured their agreement and the man walked to the bar, ordered a beer, and disappeared into the back with one of the women. Charlie was carried to the truck and left beside Paul, who was passed out. Six hours later the truck pulled up to the bunkhouse. Paul was hung over the next morning but mounted Tony and spent his day working on windmills. Charlie was unable to get out of bed.

It was a week before Charlie was well enough to hitch a ride to San Antonio and make his way to a freight car going east. Paul stayed at the ranch, unwilling to go home.

Chapter seven

With Charlie gone, Paul had no close friends on the ranch. He was a kid in a world of men. He worked hard, ate well, gained weight, and spent his off hours with his horse. Amarillo Slim was a good rider and he knew horses. He taught Paul how to get Tony to do a few tricks such as side stepping and rearing up on command, even bowing like Tony the Wonder Horse. Tony was a cow pony, a horse that had been trained to work around cattle. He was easy to ride and easy to train. Paul rode him all over the ranch and spent time washing and brushing him. He came to see the horse as his best friend.

His evenings were spent in the bunkhouse where he learned to play poker for a nickel a hand. At first, he lost most of his hands and limited his losses to a quarter a night. Five losing hands and he was out. He began to win a few hands and his poker playing went on for several hours each night but he always left down twenty-five cents. After a few weeks he was leaving with a small win, then bigger piles of coins. He discovered a talent for the game. He was smart, patient, and could control his emotions. He learned to sense the hands of the other men. He never pushed for bigger pots nor did he overplay the hands he was dealt.

He kept his winnings and his pay in a tobacco tin under his mattress. He found himself with over fifty dollars, a sum he could never imagine. He sought out

Leander Johnson and asked the ranch manager advice about what to do with it.

"Never keep more than a month's pay under your bed," Leander said. "Some of the men ain't all that trustworthy, if you get my drift. I'll keep your money in the safe and you can get it anytime you want." So Leander became Paul's banker.

Paul went to the cantina on pay nights with five silver dollars and always left drunk and broke. He awoke the following mornings hung-over and ashamed of himself for spending time with the ugly women who emptied his pockets. By autumn he was growing restless and wondering what other parts of the country looked like. He had something over one-hundred-fifty dollars in cash, a fortune to him. He promised himself that come spring he would take off. A tragedy moved up his departure.

It is widely believed that a snake cannot kill a horse. After all, it's reasoned, anti-venom is made by injecting a snake's venom into a horse's bloodstream. The amount of venom used in this process is not equal to the venom a large rattlesnake will inject into the animal in an attack that results in a bite. Horses die of rattlesnake bites in a number of ways. Most common is a bite to the nose that causes the air passages to swell, preventing the horse from breathing. Bites to the leg can produce infections that are fatal to the horse.

Tony was the victim of the most common bite. Paul and Tony were riding fence, meaning Paul was looking for sections of barbed wire that needed repair to prevent cattle from wandering away. Mesquite grew along the older fence lines and rattlesnakes seeking shade from the midday heat would crawl under the vegetation, rest, and wait for a passing rabbit or other small meal to pass by.

Horses are curious. The snake rattled a warning and Tony bent his head to the ground to see what it was. The attack was swift. By evening Tony was unable to breath and smothering. Amarillo Slim, a lifelong horse lover, could not endure the animal's suffering. He ended it with a shot from a Winchester rifle. Paul was grief stricken and unable to speak for several hours. He sat by the horse and cried. Decades later, as an old man, he would tear up in boozy moments and whisper, "A snake killed Tony."

Paul refused to choose another horse. He went to Leander Johnson and asked for his money, then he hitched a ride to San Antonio and caught a freight train heading north and west. He travelled with his cash sewn into the clothes he was wearing. He carried a small knapsack with personal items and some biscuits offered by the Mexican cooks.

He got off at Dalhart and walked along the tracks until he found a path to the hobo jungle. It was in an area of scrub brush at the end of an alley that led into the low part of town. It was his first encounter with the Dust Bowl people, the refugees from the hard times on the Great Plains. Dalhart was as bad as it got. Entire families were camped in cardboard boxes, plywood, and ragged tents made out whatever they could find. Thin, filthy children wandered among the men and women who had fled the dry land in the middle of the country. Some of them rode the rails but most just spent their days waiting; for what, no one knew.

The federal government encouraged Americans to plow up the plains in the early part of the Twentieth

Century and millions of acres of grass that had kept the land from blowing away for hundreds of years was exposed to the elements. For a few years the rain was good and the crops were plentiful but by the thirties the rain stopped, the crops dried up, and the land began to blow away in huge and hideous storms that blackened the sky for thousands of feet into the air and smothered babies and old people.

Thousands packed what they could onto whatever they could find that moved and headed out, some to California, where they were seen as vermin, and some to anywhere but the plains. Some were just stuck in places like Dalhart. Paul had never seen misery like this, not even back in Alabama in the days of corn meal and lard for dinner. They didn't beg. They didn't speak. They stared. They lived next to the hobo jungle and some of their men were planning to ride the rails looking for work while the women and children stayed in the camp and waited.

The rail yards had been built to haul the bounty of the Great Plains to a waiting world. In the Dirty Thirties there was no bounty and the trains were just passing through on their way to someplace where it still rained.

The jungle was a mass of dirty men and boys, and a few women and girls, who were flopped around fires, listening to the freight trains being put together in the yard. A man and a woman were having sex within sight of everyone else. The woman looked back at the hobos looking at her. She had no expression on her face as the man above her went to his passion. When it was over, the man rose and put himself together and handed the woman fifty cents. She took the money, pulled down her skirt, and walked to the fire where a stew was bubbling.

She gave the money to the hobo who was tending the pot and he handed her a tin bowl filled with food. She quietly walked away, found a place to sit, and ate. No one spoke to her. Paul thought it was the saddest thing he had ever witnessed. A human being allowed another person into her body so she could get something to eat.

Paul walked into the town and found a store that sold supplies for the road. He bought two surplus army blankets, two towels, two bars of soap and containers for them, and two canteens. He found a service station that had a hose, filled the canteens, and began to clean himself until a mechanic ran him off, hollering that bums were not welcome to use the hose. He went back to the camp and divided his purchases, then he walked over to the woman who had sold herself and gave her a blanket, towel, soap and container, a canteen, and five silver dollars. He walked away without saying anything. An hour later the woman was gone and he never saw her again.

Chapter eight

It was cold in Denver. Paul had grown accustomed
to the South Texas heat and he was not prepared for the
snow that fell on the hobo jungle near the freight yard on
his first night in the Rockies. October snows are
common and usually melt under the day's sunshine, but
dawn was hours away and the only comfort came from
the fires that were controlled by the older men, the ones
who shooed away the young and the weak.

A group of teenagers had set up a their own
encampment near a rusting freight car on a siding that
was no longer in use, judging by the rust on the rails.
The car's sliding door had jammed, leaving an opening
about a foot wide, and some of the kids were living in
the car. They had a fire going and a something was
bubbling in a pot. Paul walked over and introduced
himself.

A young man sporting a black eye and a scratch on
his neck was tending the pot. "You got anything to
contribute?" His voice was high and broke as he spat out
the words.

"Naw, I ain't," Paul said.

"Then you can just keep movin' cause we ain't no
charity here." The young man turned away.

Paul stood and shivered and wondered if he should
tell the boy he had some money and could buy a meal.
He had seen others attacked and robbed for much less
than he carried and he knew that there were desperate

and ruthless men in the jungle who wouldn't think twice about knifing him for dollar, much less the cash he had secreted in his clothing. He turned and walked away and found a small café that was open.

A weary-looking woman was wiping a table when he walked in. "We don't serve hobos," she said, standing and placing her hands on her hips.

"I'm just looking to get something to eat," Paul said. He looked cold, hungry and frightened.

"You got the price of dinner? We ain't got no free food here, honey."

"Yeah, I can pay."

"Let me see," she said, giving him a hard look. "You'll pay first or you'll turn right around and git."

Paul produced a silver dollar from an inside pocket and held it for her.

"Where'd you git that? You knock somebody over the head?"

"I worked for it."

"How old are you?"

Paul was hungry and tired of the talk. "I'm old enough to get a damn meal."

The woman laughed and pointed to a table near the window. "Well, you got spunk, I suppose. Have a seat."

Paul walked to the table and sat down and watched as the woman waved her behind at him. "You got more than a dollar, sweetie? I can make you feel better'n a steak dinner."

"How much is the steak?"

"Steak and fixin's happens to be exactly one dollar. I'll throw in some coffee. Then we'll see what else you'd like."

Paul spent a warm night in a bed, comforted by a woman of uncertain virtue, on a full stomach. He had even washed himself with water that was heated on the woman's wood stove, using his new soap and towel. He lay between the sheets and asked himself if he could be any happier. The woman was no beauty queen but she was several steps up from the women at the cantina and she didn't hurry him or smell bad. She seemed to like his company. She had asked him for two dollars for her and another for the privilege of spending the night in her bed. All in all, it was about the same price as the services at the cantina.

The woman snuggled against him. "You're pretty damn handsome, you know that? I bet you got all the girls you want."

"Naw, I'm not," he said, hoping that what she said was true.

"You sure are, sweetie. I know the road sisters in the jungle would like to be where I am right now, riding your rail." She laughed and climbed aboard.

He stayed with her for a week, paying by the day, until it occurred to him that she would take every cent he had and throw him out onto the street. He had caught her looking through his kit and assumed she was hoping to steal his cash, but he either wore his clothes or kept them nearby when they were both naked, so she never had the opportunity to search his clothes and find where he had stashed it. He knew he was down to something under a hundred dollars, a small fortune for the time, but he didn't chance counting it. It was time to move on.

She used a privy behind her house each morning after she climbed from her bed and he used the time she was out back to take off, leaving no note or explanation.

He was fed, warm, and clean and he was happy to leave it at that.

He walked back to the jungle by way of a small store that sold groceries and notions, and bought two tins of beef, two cans of tomatoes, a can opener, a small bottle of hot sauce, and a half-dozen candy bars. The next time he was asked to put something in the pot he wouldn't have to walk away. He went next door to a clothing store and bought a leather jacket and some wool socks.

By noon he was in a boxcar headed north, in the company of a dozen men and two women who kept to themselves and said nothing. The car was empty and smelled of some kind of fuel. Some of the other men played cards in a serious sort of way that made the game a contest. Losers shouted obscenities at the winners, who shouted back. One of the players, an older, grizzled man who had no teeth and was missing some fingers, pulled out a knife and threatened a player who had just won a hand and a few coins.

"I'll cut your dang tongue out, you cheatin' son of a bitch," he said. His eyes were red and running.

"I ain't a cheat. You're the cheat around here. Everybody knows you cheat and you're a danged yegg and more worthless than a tramp, and you ain't nothin'." Yegg was an insulting term for hobos.

"Don't you call me that, you damn fool." The older man jumped up and went after the other fellow with the knife, slicing at his eyes. The would-be victim reached into his coat and pulled out a revolver, aimed at the attacker, and fired, hitting the older man in the throat. He then dragged the man to the car's door, slid it open, and threw the dying man onto the tracks. He closed the door and went back to where he was sitting. No one said a word. The females moved closer to each other and looked away. Paul vowed to buy himself a gun.

Chapter nine

The rail lines up from Denver dropped hobos, along with the temperature, as winter approached. More rail riders were heading south than north. Those who had been through the cold months up in the northern Rockies didn't want to do it again, so they rode down to places like Texas or Arizona, or even California, where tramps were unwelcome and faced hostility and violence. By the time Paul rode into Casper, Wyoming, the freight cars were mostly empty of hobos, with a hardy few hanging on because they didn't have the gumption or the disposition to turn around. Even the rail yards and hobo jungles were mostly empty and the railroad bulls didn't bother to beat up the men they found. It was like hibernation had set in.

Paul found himself alone in an empty cattle car on a train that slowed and stopped near Bozeman, Montana, on a crisp morning in early November. He had been sleeping in a corner, wrapped in his blanket and jacket, dreaming of the woman back in Denver, when he felt the train jerk to a stop. He expected the train to move again but time passed and there was no movement and there were no voices of bulls or railroad workers along the tracks. Up ahead he heard the steam engine puffing and moving but the cattle car remained where it was.

He went to the door and pulled it back enough to see out. What he saw was the most beautiful sight he had ever seen. Clear blue sky, deep golden fields, and snow-capped mountains that reached higher than he could have imagined in a fairy tale. He was mesmerized and stood in the door and watched the sun light up the Bridger Range of the Rockies. He looked up toward the front of the train and saw that the locomotive was pulling away without the cars. The train was on a side track and was being left there. It was not unusual for surplus stock to sit for weeks or months. Paul had heard of hobos who were stranded and had to walk for miles to find food and company.

He scanned the horizon for signs of a town and guessed that one was nearby but he had no idea how far it was. He saw smoke rising from a distant house. He grabbed his kit and checked for bulls looking for tramps, saw none, and set out for the house. By midday he had reached a log ranch house set amid outbuildings and a corral where a dozen or so horses were kept. A few were moving but most were standing still and appeared to be dozing.

He slowed as he approached the house, wary of trespassing into an area where he assumed everyone was armed. He shouted, "Hello! Hello!" and received no reply. He walked up the steps to a covered porch near the front door and stepped up to knock when the door opened and an older man appeared.

"You make a habit of yelling ever' time you go someplace?" The man was Agamemnon Morrisey, known to family and friends as "Hoot." Hoot Morrisey was in his early sixties. His hair was white and thin but he could work all day and his body was as hard as the life he led. His father had been the first white man to claim the ground that now comprised a ranch of three thousand acres of owned land and a few thousand others of government grazing land.

"Hello, sir. I was wondering if you're takin' on hired hands." Paul stood on the porch with his hat in his hand and looked every inch the boy trying to wear a man's skin.

"I don't give handouts to tramps, if that's what you mean." Hoot tried to hide a smile behind his serious stare.

"No, sir. I'm not lookin' for a handout."

"Well, damn, c'mon in. We'll see." Hoot opened the door wide and stepped aside so Paul could enter.

The house was warm and a fire was burning in an oversized fireplace where cooking pots were bubbling with something that smelled wonderful to a boy who had been living out of tinned food containers. There was the scent of fresh coffee in the air. The furniture was old fashioned and seemed to Paul to be from another century, which it was. A horsehair-covered settee was positioned opposite the fireplace and two formal, velvet-covered chairs were on either side. Mahogany tables were placed next to the chairs and each had a stack of books on the top shelf. Coal oil floor lamps offered light. Paul assumed Hoot had been enjoying a book when he heard him hollering in the yard.

"You et?" Hoot asked.

"I had a little something earlier," Paul said, not wanting to appear the beggar.

"My guess is you could use a plate of stew. Am I right?"

"Yes, sir." Paul moved to the fireplace and placed his hands up to the warmth.

"Set your kit down and c'mon over to the table. We'll chow down on this son of a gun stew I got here."

Paul sat at the polished plank table and watched as Hoot filled a tin plate with steaming stew and brought it over and set it down in front of him. He returned to the fire and got a plate for himself. "Know why it's called son of a gun stew?"

"No." Paul stared at the food and wondered what was in it.

"It's called that because it's made from beef that comes from a dang steer that wandered off. Son of a gun wouldn't stay on the dang trail. There he is now, sittin' in a pile of potatoes and cabbage. Taste it."

Paul took a mouthful and found the beef tender but bland. He had been dousing his food with hot sauce to make it edible and the plain beef and potatoes had no taste at all to him. "Good," he said.

Hoot could tell that Paul was not pleased. "Dang, boy, I'd a thought you'd be diggin' in."

"I usually put hot sauce in my food." Paul felt embarrassed to be having this conversation with a kind man who had offered him a meal.

"Well, get it out and let's have at it," Hoot said.

Both of them finished their stew with red faces. "Dang, it sure does spice it up," Hoot said, taking a long pull of water. "Let's clean this up and we can have a talk about your future."

The fire, the meal, a feeling of safety, and a comfortable chair had Paul nodding off as Hoot packed his pipe. The older man looked at the boy, lit his pipe, and went back to his book. Two hours later Paul came around and saw Hoot smiling at him.

"Where you from, boy?"

"I'm from Alabama but I've been on the road for awhile."

"Life hard back there?

"Life's hard ever'where, seems like."

"If you're lookin' for work, I got it," Hoot said. "I got cattle need lookin' after and most of my hired men ran off for the winter. I could use help but I got no use for man or boy doesn't pull their weight. I don't have a charity operation here." He gave Paul a hard look.

"I can work. I worked on a ranch in Texas and did fine."

"You punch cattle down there?"

"Windmills, mostly."

"We got plenty of water and don't need 'em here but I got cattle winterin' over and it's damn hard work and it's damn cold at times. Twenty dollars a month, room and board if you're up to it."

"That's what I got in Texas and it'll be fine."

"Why'd you leave Texas?"

"Snake killed my horse." Paul looked into the fire and his eyes misted.

"Horses die, son, just like people. You need to move on. Come with me, I'll show you the place." Hoot walked into a room at the back of the house and motioned for Paul to follow him. The room was lined with shelves floor to ceiling. The shelves were filled with books. "Have you read Moby Dick?"

"Yes, sir."

"How about Shakespeare? Read anything of his?"

"A teacher read something of his to us. Hamlet, I think."

"I have the classics here, son. Not all of them are in English. Some are German or French. I want you to promise me something. We work six days a week here. Every man gets one day to himself. I want you to promise me that you will read on your day off. You don't have to read all day but I want you to come in here, choose a book, and read it. Deal?"

Hoot had no way of knowing that Paul's secret desire, one he had never allowed himself to believe would come to pass, was to have access to books. He had loved reading since he was a small boy listening to Sarah read to him and he walked around Hoot's library, touching the volumes. "Yes, sir."

Chapter ten

Hoot Morrisey was as close to a father as Paul ever had. The man ran the ranch as a benevolent dictator, quick to smile when things went according to his plan and quick to anger when they didn't. He showed his hired hands what he wanted done and expected that it would be. It was not unusual to see a man sent packing when Hoot decided that the fellow wasn't up to whatever task he had been assigned. He allowed no alcohol to be consumed in the bunkhouse and there were no women on the ranch, not even the cooks. His wife had died some years earlier and she had been the last female to reside on the land he controlled. The hired men considered him odd for a rancher and snickered behind his back that he was too fancy for his own good.

Paul was considered Hoot's "boy" and the older men razzed him about the time he spent reading. The feeling among the ranch hands was that too much reading was bad for a man and led to softness and even feminine ways. New hands saw Paul as an easy way to assert their manliness and they picked fights with him.

A cowhand who called himself Cat kept a supply of whiskey behind a wood pile at the back of the bunk house. Hoot had heard rumors but hadn't done any investigating, figuring the truth would surface sooner or later. Most of the men stayed at the ranch on their days off because Hoot did not provide transportation to Bozeman or any other town or crossroads where entertainment of a cowboy nature could be found. If one of his hired men could make his way into town, he had no problem with it, assuming the man made it back for his work the following morning at dawn. Cat was a man who believed that life's purpose was a good time. For him, that meant women and liquor. If he couldn't have one, he'd have the other.

And so Cat was playing cards with the other men and taking trips to the wood pile on a bone chilling night and observing Paul on his bunk reading. When Paul read, he folded his right arm up and under his head, and held the book in his left hand. He had a habit of grinding his back teeth while he scanned the pages, causing his jaw muscles to flex. As Cat got drunker he decided that Paul was getting on his nerves.

"You're goddam jaws are bouncing outta your face, you know that?"

Paul ignored him and kept reading.

"You hear me, you Hillbilly. You're drivin' me nuts with your readin' and jaw bouncin'."

Paul didn't bother to look up.

Cat paced in front of Paul's bed and his face got red. He moved to him and grabbed the book out of Paul's hand and threw it across the room. Paul looked up at him and sprang into his face, pummeling the older man with his fists. The rage was not controllable and whatever had been kept under lock in Paul's emotions came out. It took three men to pull Paul off of Cat, whose face was bloody. Red drool came from his mouth and his eyes were unfocused. When word got back to Hoot, he said, "Cat had it comin'." Then he fired Cat.

A second incident involved a knife. All of the men carried hunting or skinning knives that they kept sharp as razors. Hoot allowed the men to keep and sell the skins of varmints they killed, mostly coyotes, foxes, and small ground dwellers. Hoot kept rights to all wolf hides. The beating Paul gave Cat caused the other men to steer clear of fistfights with him. A cowboy who grandly called himself Oklahoma Bob got to drinking on his day off and went after Paul with his six-inch hunting knife. Oklahoma Bob was unaware that Paul, as a boy, entertained himself with knives and could throw a balanced knife like a circus performer.

Oklahoma Bob built up his courage as he pulled down the whiskey and walked up to Paul and shoved him. "Hey, Mister Reader, I think you're a fancy man."

"Fuck you," said Paul

"Don't nobody say that to me, Mister Fancy." He pulled the knife out of its leather holder and held it in front of Paul's face. The rage that had sent him into Cat returned but he knew that flying into Oklahoma Bob face would get him stabbed.

Paul backed up and reached under his mattress. Seconds later, Oklahoma Bob was screaming and staring at blade sticking out of his leg. Paul walked over, pulled out the knife, wiped it on Oklahoma Bob's pants, and put it in his belt. Again, Hoot sided with Paul and Oklahoma Bob was last seen carrying his kit down the lane, limping and using a stick as a cane.

Other men thought he had fire but was lacking in real knowledge of the manly arts. They gave up their teasing and took him to school in their own way. By his seventeenth birthday he was good with his fists and even better with a knife. Old hands who had been in hard places taught him how to hold a knife in a fight and how and where to attack. More than one man carried a scar from these encounters and others had lost teeth to Paul's fists. It surprised him that a deep well of anger from his childhood could be plumbed in these struggles and he was delighted at how good he felt after he had beaten a man. He was also ashamed.

While his body grew strong and hard; his mind grew at an even faster pace. He discovered that he could remember entire passages of books after reading them for the first time. He would read a scene from Hamlet, close the book, and recite the scene. A student of Shakespeare, someone who had seen the great British actors on the stage, would laugh out loud at Paul's backwoods recitation of Hamlet's line, *Excellent, I' faith, of the chameleon's dish: I eat the air, promise-cramm'd—you cannot feed capons so.* Out of Paul's mouth it was, "Excellent, ah faith, of the chameleon's (pronouncing the ch) dish, Ah oyt the ear, promise cram dee, you cain't feed capons so." None of the cow punchers knew the difference and thought Paul was speaking a foreign language, probably French, they mumbled, and winked at each other, and assumed that men who spoke French were homosexuals.

He read Plato, Dumas and Dickens and spent evenings with Hoot discussing the books and what they meant. He listened as Hoot advised him to spend his life offering compassion to the good and the weak and swift and merciless justice to the wicked. Hoot's personal philosophy was simple and it was based on the frontier idea of everyone pulling their own weight. "There's them and there's us," he said. "Us is the good ones. Them are bad. You're with me or against me. It ain't that hard to figure out."

Hoot believed that a man working on a ranch should be armed and he provided handguns and rifles to his hired men if they didn't have guns of their own. He had purchased two cases of single action Colt .45 revolvers from surplus U.S. Army stocks after World War One and kept them for his ranch hands to use. The army had switched to a semi-automatic version of the .45 and was shedding its revolvers. He also had a supply of Winchester rifles. The firearms were to be used against the wolves that threatened the livestock, injured or sick cattle, and any other emergency that required lethal force.

Paul had been using firearms nearly all his life. He didn't care for the Colt .45 because of its large caliber kick and asked for and did not receive a smaller handgun. "You aint' gonna bring a wolf down with a pea shooter," Hoot said. "If you're old enough to be cow punching you're man enough to fire it."

The winter before he turned eighteen was bitter in Montana, even by local standards. Cattle froze to death where they stood and wolves were aggressive in their search for something to eat. Hoot sent his hands out to ride fence and find the spots where cattle could wander off into the mountains and be lost. Cattle that could be rounded up were brought in closer to the barns where hay was available to feed them.

It was hard, cold work and Paul worried that he would freeze to death along with the cattle. He rode one of the ranch horses in his work, no longer allowing himself to become attached to any of them. He often rotated among the available animals, choosing a gentle mare one day and a spirited stallion the next. He went out wrapped in a sheepskin coat, a slicker, a scarf around his head, and sheepskin gloves on his hands. He carried his .45 in his coat and the Winchester in a case attached to the saddle. He carried several lengths of ropes, wire cutters, a hammer, and nails to be used to repair fences.

On a January morning in 1939, Paul set out with two other men just as the winter sun was lightening the sky to the east. They followed a path that had been made by other men the day before. The snow was nearly two feet deep and the temperature was below zero. The Montana wind caused exposed skin to ache.

They traveled one behind the other, with Paul last. The wind all but drowned out the sound of the horses. After an hour or so the men came to a place where the fence crossed a creek, now frozen. The east side of the fence was ranch land, the west side was federal grazing land that was open to adjoining ranches and where cattle were mixed and would need to be sorted when the weather was better. Hoot liked to keep his cattle close at hand and wanted the fence checked for breaks that would allow his stock to mix in with others on the western side.

The men spread out, some searching for cattle to bring in; others, including Paul, riding the fence. He moved along at a slow pace with his eye on the barbed wire, hoping there were no breaks that would force him to get down from the horse and use his tools to make repairs. He found a spot where the barbed wire was on the ground. It had been pulled away from the posts on each end of the section, mostly likely by a steer pushing against it. Paul idly wondered why a steer would do that when he saw the wolf. It was standing over a dead steer that was down in the snow and partially covered. The animal's neck was open where the wolf had eaten.

The wolf looked up at Paul and snarled, baring its teeth. Without thinking, Paul removed his glove and reached inside his coat for the Colt. He pulled the .45 out, pulled back the hammer, and aimed at the wolf, hitting it in the mouth. There was a quick yelp and the wolf was down. It trembled for a few seconds and lay still as Paul kept the revolver aimed at it, ready to fire again should the animal jump up to attack. He saw no movement so he urged the horse across the downed barbed wire and over to where the wolf lay near the dead steer. He sat on the horse and kept the gun aimed low until he was satisfied that the wolf was dead.

Hoot wanted proof of dead wolves because he offered his hired men a five dollar bonus for each one they brought in. Paul put the gun back in his coat but he couldn't let go because it was frozen to his hand. His mistake had been removing his glove. He waited for his jacket to warm his hand so he could put his glove back on but it his skin was in a hard freeze against the weapon. He managed to climb down from the horse, pick up the wolf by its tail, and drape it over the saddle for the ride back to the bunk house.

It was nearly noon before his hand was separated from the Colt and by then some of his palm had been torn and pulled away from the flesh underneath. Hoot rubbed a salve on Paul's hand and wrapped it in gauze. He then gave Paul five silver dollars. "Next time you might want to keep your glove on," he said.

Chapter eleven

It was spring before Paul's hand was fully healed. Hoot allowed no excuses to avoid the work that needed to be done, not injury and not illness. A man could either work or he couldn't. If he couldn't, he should expect to be let go, or at least be off the payroll until he could pull his weight. So Paul kept his hand wrapped and did what was expected of him, fixing fences and punching cattle. He took the time to learn to shoot with his left hand. He worked his way through Hoot's library of classic Greek literature and could recite *The Iliad* to the cowboys who were at once fascinated and confused. His recitation was flavored with a thick Southern accent and some of the men assumed that this Homer fellow must have been from Alabama, where strange things take place.

The bitter winter had left Hoot's herd thin and scattered and the first of the warmer days were spent rounding up strays and counting heads. The warm breezes that flowed across the grazing land gave Paul the urge to move on. He had spent nearly four years on the ranch, growing taller and stronger. He had saved several hundred dollars, a fortune to him and most others during those hard years. His savings were mostly the result of Hoot's policy of making it hard for cowboys to get to town to spend their money. Hoot, like Leander Johnson, paid his young cowboys in silver dollars and Paul had piles of them stored in cigar boxes in Hoot's safe.

He took a deep breath and broke the news. "I'm thinkin' of movin' on," he said. "Might be time for me to see some other part of the country."

Hoot had been expecting it and smiled. "It's not as easy out there as it is here."

"What's easy about this?" Paul was thinking about the back-breaking work on the ranch.

"You get fed. You get paid. You got people who are your friends. You know it wasn't like that when you walked up the road to this place."

"Well, I know you've been good to me, but a man's got to see what's out there."

"So he does. How'd you like your pay? You ain't plannin' to walk out of here with all that silver, are you?"

"Paper money would be good." Paul was choking up at the thought of leaving.

"Where to?"

"I'm thinking of visiting Oregon. I hear it's nice there."

"That it is. They got some nice ranchland and mountains, just like we got here in Montana."

"I'm thinkin' my cow punchin' days are over. I'd like to try something a little more indoors."

Hoot laughed. "Hell, boy. That's the first thing you've said in a while that makes sense." He slapped his knee. "Yes, sir, try something indoors." He stared at Paul and a big smile spread across his face. "I might have something you'd be interested in. You can't tell nobody about this and you'll have to promise before I'll say any more."

Paul leaned forward and was surprised to see Hoot grinning like a boy. "I promise."

"Here's the deal. I know someone who's in need of a reliable man who's good with his fists and knows how to shoot but ain't hot headed. Somebody who can control a situation, if you get my drift."

"No, I don't think I do."

"I know you can fight and I know you can shoot and hit what you aim at. I've seen you deal with these cowboys and their ways. There's a need for men like you, as young as you are. What I'm sayin' is this. I know where you can get a job maintaining order in a certain establishment in Medford, Oregon. Pay's better'n here and the work's indoors. My guess is you'd like the company." Hoot's eyes were bright and he raised his eyebrows in a question.

"What kind of establishment?" Paul was confused at Hoot's demeanor and whatever he was trying to say.

"It's a whorehouse!" Hoot let out a loud laugh and slapped his knee.

"That ain't funny," Paul said. "I thought you were serious."

"Hell, boy. I am serious. I won't go into the details but I happen to know a woman who owns the place and she's always writin' to say she can't get reliable men to keep order. Drunks and bums show up at her door and they get rowdy. Some of them get rough with the girls. You're young and handsome and you'd look good in a suit, I'd guess, and all you'll have to do is knock a few heads now and then."

Paul was nearly nineteen and the word "whorehouse" was enough to send him into a blizzard of fantasies, all of them lurid enough to send his hormones into maximum saturation. His first thought was not about the work of a bouncer in such a place, it was about what the girls looked like and what they did behind closed doors, which, in his imagination, was everything, whatever it was.

Hoot drove one of his trucks into Bozeman, where Paul used some of his money to buy a ticket on a passenger train. He went into a dry goods store and purchased a suit that more or less fit. Paul had skinny legs, a twenty-nine inch waist, and wide shoulders. As he would learn, suits came with pants and jackets. For Paul, either the pants were too big or the jacket was too small. There were no skilled tailors in Bozeman at the time, so he travelled in pants that looked as though they belonged to someone else.

He had never travelled in a passenger car. He stared at the other passengers, who knew a cowboy when they saw one. He offered a goofy smile and "howdy" to everyone he passed and even removed his hat to each and every female who made eye contact with him, even those who made it plain that they thought he was uncouth and should be riding in a cattle car. They, of course, had no way of knowing that he had arrived in Montana in such a way.

He went to the dining car and enjoyed a steak dinner in the company of a travelling salesman who didn't bother to engage in conversation with someone who had "hick" written all over him. He dozed in his seat, keeping his small suitcase tight against his body. He had his money secreted in his clothes and in his shoes and a robber would have had to leave him naked to get away with all that Paul had saved while he worked for Hoot. Paul's only regret was that he didn't have a gun to protect himself should someone try to rob him. He kept a skinning knife on his belt and a folding knife in his pocket, but knew that it wouldn't be enough against someone with a .45.

Late the following day, after changing trains twice, Paul gazed at the town of Medford, home to something around fifteen thousand people who served the needs of fruit and lumber businesses throughout the region in a place called the Rogue Valley. Medford is drier than other parts of Oregon and enjoyed an agreeable climate. Paul was startled to see a sign at the depot saying, "Welcome to Medford, County Seat of Jackson County." He had a brief vision of the Jackson County where he grew up and wondered how many counties in United States were named after the man.

He left the train holding his suitcase to his chest with one hand and his pants up with the other. Hoot had given him an address and he hoped it would be within sight of the depot. It took him two hours of wandering around the small town before he found it with the aid of a helpful policeman who looked at the address and smiled. "Pauline's. Everybody knows where Pauline's is."

It was nearly dark when Paul walked up to the gray Victorian house. Everything was gray. The brick, the porch, the fancy woodwork, even the windows were painted gray. No light was visible from the street. It was dark and quiet. A small painted sign on the front door advised visitors to "Use the back door." He went around back and knocked on a door whose window was painted gray.

"Who is it?" A voice came from inside.

"Paul Brite. I'm here to see Pauline."

There was the sound of locks being worked and the door opened. There, in a silk kimono, was a big, smiling woman who had the tallest and reddest hairdo Paul had ever seen. She also had large breasts that were on prominent display without any visible means of support. "That'd be me," she said. "C'mon in and don't let your tongue hang out." Her laugh was loud and free and Paul wondered if he had died and gone to heaven.

He walked into a Victorian parlor, with red, flocked wallpaper, fringed electric lamps, an oriental rug, and velvet-covered chairs and settees. Paintings on the wall were of naked fat women lying on fur rugs.

"You'll get used to it," Pauline said.

No I won't, he thought.

Chapter twelve

Pauline led Paul into the kitchen, where a half-dozen young women were sitting around a table eating dinner. The women looked up when Paul entered and a couple of them smiled at him.

"Ladies, this here is Paul. Paul and Pauline. We're a team, I suppose. He's our new goon. A friend says he can handle himself and we'll see if he can handle some of our rowdy boys."

One of the women looked up and pointed to Paul. "I'll handle him if he can't handle himself." The others snickered at the joke.

"Ain't nobody gonna handle this boy, you hear me. He's on the job."

"Yes, ma'am," they murmured, giggling.

"You hungry?" Pauline looked at Paul and pointed to a pot of chicken and dumplings on the stove.

"Yes, ma'am, I am."

"Don't you call me ma'am. I ain't your ma. Call me Pauline. Get yourself a plate. When you're done meet me in the parlor. We can talk about a few things."

Paul sat at the table with the girls and ate, catching glances at them glancing at him. They were about his age, he guessed, but it was hard to tell with all the makeup they wore. A couple of them looked more like mannequins than real people. They wore white powder on their faces with large red circles on their cheeks and blue eye makeup. Their lipstick was bright red and thick. He was both attracted to them and repelled. One of the girls was very pretty and had almost no makeup. She was wearing a schoolgirl's uniform. Another woman, who appeared to be the oldest, was wearing a beaded dress and a headband.

"Where you from?" asked the schoolgirl.

"I'm from Alabama but I've been working in Montana."

"You been working in a whorehouse?" asked the woman in the beaded dress.

"Cow punchin', mostly."

"Hey, let's get this show on the road!" Pauline yelled from the parlor. "We got business coming soon. Eat up and get ready. You, Paul, c'mon in here."

Paul wolfed down the last of his dinner, set his plate in the sink with the others, and waved to the girls.

"Here's how it works, Sport," Pauline said, by way of opening the conversation. "You get twenty-five a week. I take back five for your room and board. And no you don't have the choice of livin' someplace else. We need a man around all day and all night and right now you're it. You stay away from the girls during business hours. What you and they do during their off time is not my concern unless it gets in the way. You get my drift? Don't fall in love. Don't get jealous. Some of the boys that come in here might get rough with the girls or start trouble. Your job is to get them outta here. I don't care how you do it as long as you don't do nothin' that brings the police or the newspapermen. The police are agreeable to most things. I have an understanding with them, if you get my drift again. That understanding does not extend to shooting people who ain't shooting back or leaving somebody crippled enough to come around askin' for money." She sat back and took a breath. "That about covers it."

"When do I start?"

"You're started, Sport. Where's your gun? I want you to wear your gun out where customers can see it."

"I don't have a gun."

"How can you be my goon if you ain't armed? Do I have to do everything?" She shook her head and tried to frown but a smile came over her face. Pauline went upstairs and came back with a small handgun that looked like a toy. "This is for my personal protection. You can carry it tonight but you're going to get your own gun tomorrow and I want to see something that'll scare the shit of people, nothing like this here." She handed him the small pistol.

It was a weeknight and was slow, at least in Pauline's judgment. Between dinner and midnight, a half-dozen men walked through the back door, all of them sober. They glanced at Paul and each man, in his turn, asked, "Who's he?"

"My new goon," Pauline responded. "He's here to kick your ass if you get outta line."

Most of the customers smiled and muttered something about Paul not looking much like a goon, with his too-large pants and too-small pistol. No one made trouble and the night passed.

Paul's room was a small, closet-size space on the third floor of the house; a semi-finished portion of the attic. His bunk was crammed against a wall and blocked the only part of the room where he could stand up. The roof supports formed the ceiling and pitched in on either side, forcing him to stoop to get to the bed. Below his room were the girls' rooms, where they entertained customers and lived. The floor of his room was the ceiling of theirs. He could hear everything. On this first night he was excited to listen to their conversations. They talked about their customers and their quirks and they talked about him, mostly in positive, physical terms. It was nearly dawn before he fell into sleep and was woken by pounding on his door in late morning.

"Hey, goon, you gonna sleep away the day?" It was Pauline.

"Be right down," he said, in a Southern accent that was thickened by sleep. Pauline didn't understand a word of it but she was happy to get a response.

He used a second floor bathroom that was filled with items he had never seen before; rubber bags and hoses, creams and lotions, black garters, see-through undergarments and all kinds of clips and pins. He was pleased that the sink offered hot water and he refreshed himself with soap that smelled like perfume. He brushed his teeth using baking soda he found on a shelf. He wet his hair and combed it straight back, exposing a widow's peak on his forehead. He saw in the mirror a young man who was quite pleased with himself. He was a long way from Sarah's sorry farm.

Pauline offered thick oat meal for breakfast washed down by boiled coffee made from beans she had roasted in her gas oven. The coffee was strong and bitter. "This'll take the sleep outta your head and put some lead in your pencil," she said.

"You sure you want him walkin' around with lead in his pencil," a girl named Natty said."You ain't the one's gotta get the lead out." The other girls laughed.

Pauline ignored her. "So, goon, you need to get into town and get a gun that'll do some good. While you're out get some clothes that fit. I want you lookin' good and mean. Good means snazzy clothes. I want you lookin' like a handsome and dangerous gangster."

"I like me a dangerous man," Natty said, winking at Paul. She had no makeup on her face and in the morning light she looked like any pretty young woman in church. Paul noticed that she had freckles and blue eyes. He wondered if she would go on a picnic with him and wear a big straw hat and sit on a checkered blanket like in the movies. For a moment he had a fantasy in which he sang a cowboy song to her while she blushed and looked at him in admiration. Just as quickly, the fantasy went away and he remembered what she did with her evenings and how she had looked the night before with her painted like a cartoon.

"I ain't dangerous," he said. His tone was petulant.

Chapter thirteen

The Great Depression created an economy that was based on used items. As people grew poorer they sold off what they didn't need and, after a few years, they sold off what they did need but couldn't eat. They sold their furniture, their clothing, their family heirlooms, anything that would bring enough money to allow them to survive. Pawn shops and used items stores were part of the landscape of the countryside and part of commercial life of towns and cities. Medford was no exception.

Paul found a pawnshop within two blocks of Pauline's and saw a sign in the window that said, "Guns." The man behind the counter had the look of someone who ready for a fistfight. He wore a pistol on his belt and a scowl on his face. His hands were balled into fists as he watched Paul approach. "What the hell do you want?"

"Lookin' for gun," Paul said.

"For what?"

Paul's attitude changed from friendly to hostile but he was aware that the other man was armed and he was not. He wanted to tell the man that he needed a gun so he could rob him and shoot him but his better sense kept check on him. A joke about a robbery was not a good idea at the moment. "I just need something is all."

"For what?"

"I'm sort of a guard, you might say."

"You work for Pauline?" The man's face softened.

"Yes, sir."

"Well, hell, then. Why'n't you say so." The scowl was replaced by a smile and an offered hand.

"I don't know." Paul was confused.

"Sorry about the reception. You wouldn't believe what walks in here. I've had to knock a few heads. We get chiselers and bums in this place lookin' for an easy mark. That ain't me, no sir."

"I need a large handgun."

"I'll bet you do. What do you like? Revolver or automatic? I got an Army .45 automatic here. Lots of stopping power and it's easy to shoot."

Paul still saw himself as a junior Tom Mix and he was thinking of something that a cowboy hero would carry. "You got any Colt Peacemakers?" The Peacemaker was the classic cowboy sidearm.

"You just wait 'til you see what I got for you." The man unlocked a drawer and removed a handgun that Paul fell in love with on first sight. It was a Colt 38/40. The gun had a seven-and-a-half inch barrel, was nickel-plated, and had the look of a pistol that a cowboy hero would carry in a gunfight with evil men. "Made in the 1890s and still shoots like a dream. You want to hold it?"

Paul took the gun in his hand and worked the action. He spun the cylinder and opened and closed the access that allowed the gun to be loaded and unloaded. He cocked the single-action hammer and noted that it had a fixed firing pin. He knew that meant the gun should be carried with only five rounds because an empty chamber was required as a safety measure to prevent the firing pin from setting off the round it was pressed against should the weapon be dropped. The gun was clean and well cared for, even though there were worn spots and light scratches here and there.

"How much?" he asked. At that moment he didn't care if it cost everything he had.

"Twenty dollars and it's yours."

"You got any ammo?"

"Two dollars a box. Fifty rounds."

"I'll take the gun and two boxes."

"You can walk out behind the store to fire it. There's a hill back there and some trees. You can fire a few rounds to get the feel of it if you like."

Paul went through one-hundred rounds falling in love with the big gun. He had never owned anything like it and had moments when he thought it was a dream. He fired, unloaded, re-loaded, and fired again, hitting cans, remnants of bottles, bits of paper, small branches and anything he could aim at. He went back to the pawn shop and bought two more boxes of shells.He made a promise to himself that he would never give up the weapon, no matter what happened to him and how much he needed money. It was a promise he would keep until the day he died.

By dinner time Paul was well-armed, well-dressed, and well-shod. He had spent fifty dollars, more money that he could ever imagine spending in a day. He had found a tailor who made his pants fit. He also had a new suit tailored to his body, three snazzy shirts and ties, two-toned black and white shoes, a brown fedora with a feather in the hatband, a haircut, and a large revolver in his waistband.

He had never felt better or more important. He walked into Pauline's with a smile on his face and stood in the doorway to be admired. Pauline broke into wild laughter.

"All you need is a thin little pussy bumper mustache and you'd be a right proper pimp," she said.

The girls gathered around and smiled, touching his new suit and pointing to the feather in his hat. One of them began singing Yankee Doodle and the others joined in. "…put a feather in his hat and called it macaroni."

Paul stormed up to his room and sat on his bed, feeling humiliated. Pauline climbed the steps and knocked on his door. "Hey, sport, in case you ain't figured it out, this ain't the most refined place on earth. Get your ass downstairs. We got customers."

He spent the evening sitting and sulking, and making a show of his Colt. Everyone, customers and girls, steered clear of him. He looked like what he was: a well-armed teenager with an attitude. There was no trouble that night, even though a few of the customers were drunk and became angry when it was obvious they were too far gone to do what they had come to do. Pauline offered no refunds.

Saturday night was Pauline's big payday. The lumbermen and farm workers got paid and came to town looking for a good time. They had spent the week in back-breaking, dangerous jobs and they wanted to let off a little steam. Some were ordinary men with ordinary urges. Others were the type to find satisfaction in the pain of others in the belief that transferring their own pain would somehow make it better. Some of these men frequented Pauline's and were the source of the trouble that had threatened to close it down on more than one occasion.

Lumbermen spent their working lives handling logs and machinery that could kill them in an instant. Life and death were pressed against each other and lost their distinction for some of the men. Danger had no meaning. Breathe in. Breathe out. That's about all there was to life. Pleasure today. Pain tomorrow.

A man named Jack Poultier was a patron at Pauline's. He was a regular customer and he was a regular problem. He was such a problem that Pauline demanded that he pay double for every service he sought. Jack Poultier was the reason Pauline had an opening for a bouncer, the previous occupant of the job having been hospitalized with several broken bones and a split skull.

Saturday night was Jack's time to howl. He and some of his rowdy friends would get tanked up on whiskey, climb into a flatbed truck, and head to town. Around ten o'clock they would knock on Pauline's door and barge in demanding female company of the kind found in such places. Jack believed that men were put on earth to force women to do things of a physical nature and he paid extra for the services of a woman named Delia, whose tolerance for the unusual was high. Delia was nearing forty and had, by her own admission, see and done it all. In fact, her only customers these days were the men who had a taste for things the other women refused to engage in. She had hard miles on her and it showed, right down to her ill-fitting false teeth that clattered when she spoke.

Paul's first Saturday night began tamely enough, with a few drunks mouthing off but nothing serious.

When Jack Poultier and his friends walked in, things changed. Jack was a big man with a heavy beard. He was not much given to personal hygiene and Pauline attempted to mute Jack's presence by liberally spraying the parlor with perfume. It only made the room closer and more oppressive. Paul was sitting in a chair near the corner where Delia was teaching him to smoke cigarettes. She told him it made him look older and distinguished and he coughed his way through a half dozen of them, producing a cloud of smoke that competed with the perfume and Jack Poultier's aroma, mixed with the scents of lumberjacks, farmers, and the whores who were waiting to take their money.

Jack saw Delia sitting with Paul, stormed over, and grabbed her by her wrist, jerking her up and smacking her across the face. Delia screamed and Jack smacked her again. Paul was startled at first and sat staring at Jack, but the second smack got him up from his chair.

"What the hell! You leave her alone," he said, placing himself between Jack and Delia.

Jack looked down at Paul, who was a good half a foot shorter, and shoved him back into the chair. "Get the hell out of here, boy, or you'll find your head cracked open."

Pauline tried to intervene but Jack brushed her back. The other men and women in the room just stared at Jack, but said nothing.

"Delia's my whore and I'll do what I came to do. Ain't you nor anybody else gonna stop me." He glared at Paul. "That means you, pissant." He grabbed Delia by an arm and began to drag her through the room to the stairs.

Paul heard a rushing in his ears and pressed his lips together. He was up and on Jack before the big man could turn around to face him. Paul punched Jack in the middle of his back, causing him to lose his breath. Jack released Delia, took a deep breath, and turned to face Paul with the intention of giving him a beating. Instead, he was met by the Colt, which Paul used as a club against the side of Jack's head, splitting a line from Jack's left eye to his ear and sending the big man to the floor, unconscious. Jack lay still and bleeding. Paul rolled him onto his back and waited for him to come around, which took a few minutes. When Jack opened his eyes he looked into the barrel of the big revolver and saw the cylinder rotate as Paul pulled the hammer back.

"I aim to blow your face out the back of your head," Paul said. "Do you have any last words?"

Jack tried to speak but Paul shoved the barrel into his mouth. "I'm sorry. Did you say something?" Paul was not smiling and Jack saw murder in Paul's gray eyes.

Jack shook his head and looked around for some to help him. No one stepped forward. Pauline had her hand to her mouth and waited for Paul to pull the trigger.

"Here's what's gonna happen," Paul said. "You're gonna get up and apologize to the lady and then you and your friends are gonna walk outta here and never come back. If you do I'll blow your nuts off. Understand?

Jack's head hurt and he was dizzy but he had enough presence of mind to nod in agreement. Five minutes later the rowdy men were gone along with other customers, leaving only a few farmers upstairs with the girls. Paul began to calm down and went over to Delia to comfort her. She looked up at him and slapped his face.

"You son of a bitch," she said. "You cost me thirty dollars. Next time mind your own damn business."

Pauline pulled him into the kitchen. "You ain't getting' paid this month. In case you were wonderin', your job ain't to drive customers away. How long do you think it will take for me to get Jack back in here?"

"He was hurting her," Paul said.

"That's what she gets paid for, sport. You get paid to stand around with a gun and look mean. That don't mean you get to beat up them that got the cash. Now get back out there and look like you can earn your keep."

The 1940's

Chapter fourteen

"Older men declare war. But it is youth that must fight and die." Herbert Hoover

New Year's Eve in 1939 was a grand time in Chattanooga. The Dirty Thirties were over at last and people were working again. The Tennessee Valley Authority was running lines throughout the South and providing the region with good paying jobs and electricity. War was raging in Europe and the United States was sending supplies overseas and building up its own war-making capacity and that was jobs, jobs, and more jobs. It was not boom times but it was a hell of a lot better than it had been.

Paul rode into the Chattanooga train station in style. He was wearing a fancy suit with all the trimmings. He wore a Bulova watch on his wrist and a Stetson hat on his head. And he had money in his pocket. He had quit Pauline's to come home and he planned the make the most of it. A few months working in a whorehouse had given him a new perspective on how people got through life. He had even grown used to the idea that some women made a living by letting mean men beat them or dress them up as little girls. Everybody lived with evil and everybody lived with misery. It was what happened in between these things that mattered and he planned the make the most of it.

He had purchased a sleeper-class ticket for the ride home and had eaten at tables with white tablecloths and fine china in the dining car. He had a cocky smile on his face as he stepped down from the train. He carried a leather suitcase in which was contained another suit of clothes and his 38/40. The station was crowded with men, women, and children in a mood to celebrate the coming of a new decade. He was a little drunk as he walked down the platform, having taken a few nips from a silver flask he'd picked up at the Medford pawn shop.

There to meet him was his "uncle" Charlie and his sister Elizabeth, who cried and squealed when she saw the dandy he had become. Elizabeth had grown into a beautiful teenage girl with dark hair to her shoulders and high cheekbones over an easy, open smile. She was not much over five feet tall and Paul looked down at her face as she kissed his cheek.

Charlie hadn't changed and was wearing cheap clothes that had the look of a street hustler. He wore a pork pie hat, checkered suit, and worn leather shoes peeking out from imitation leather spats. He looked like a man who was eager to offer a tip on a horse race. Paul laughed and shook Charlie's hand.

"You ain't the scruffy boy I left in Texas," Charlie said. "What happened? You hit the jackpot somewhere?"

"Been working is all," Paul said, putting his arm around his sister. "What you been up to?"

"I'm a singer. I sing with a band. I even been on the radio."

"You still in school?"

"You bet! But I'm more interested in singin'."

Charlie was driving a beat up Chevrolet that stalled at intersections and smelled like someone had thrown up bad whiskey in it. Paul sat in the back with Elizabeth and opened the window, hoping the cold air would make the ride bearable. Chattanooga is a mountain city and the old Chevy struggled up the hills and coughed black smoke as Charlie downshifted to first gear to keep it moving. He pulled up in front of a small frame house and allowed the motor to die.

"Here we are," he said, pointing to the house.

"Where's here?" Paul asked.

"This is where Mary lives. You'll be staying with her."

"What about you? Why can't I stay with you?" Paul had no desire to see his mother.

"I'm stayin' with someone and she ain't willin' to share the bed, if you know what I'm sayin'," Charlie said.

"What about you?" Paul turned to Elizabeth.

"I'm here with Mama and Herbert."

"Who's Herbert?"

"Momma's new husband."

"What's he like?"

"Like the others, only he wears glasses. You'll meet him soon enough."

Mary was waiting in the doorway when Paul and Elizabeth walked up onto the porch, which was tilting to one side because the stacked stones holding it up had slipped. She offered no affection to her children.

"I hope you got some cash," she said by way of greeting. "We could use a little something around here."

Herbert was sitting in an overstuffed chair, smoking a cigarette and reading the paper. He didn't bother to look up as Paul and Elizabeth walked in.

"That there's Herbert," Mary said. "We're married."

Paul's good mood vanished. He wanted to grab his sister and find a better place to stay. "I won't be stayin' long," he said. "Just came by to say hello."

"The hell you won't," Mary said. "We ain't been waitin' for you so's you could give us no never mind. Besides, we ain't got no money. You're lookin' good, all fancy and dressed up. Whyn't we go out on the town. Hell, it's New Year's Eve. Ain't that right, Herbert."

Herbert looked up from his paper and stared at Paul. He had a smirk that said he had plans for the money that Paul had brought home. As it turned out, everyone did.

Paul paid the bills and bought the booze for two months. By the end of February he was broke and his mother and Herbert harangued him to do something to get money. Neither of them worked or made any effort at income. Herbert claimed he had to "lay low" because "people" were after him about a misunderstanding on one thing or another. Mary backed him up and mentioned that the two of them had to hide out down by the Tennessee River for a few weeks back when the weather was warm.

Elizabeth had developed a way of coping by ignoring what was happening around her. When she was home she spent her time alone. At school or with musicians, she sang and laughed. She confided in Paul that she was making plans to head out to parts unknown and do as he did. He made her promise not to work in a whorehouse, even as a bouncer.

Chapter fifteen

Paul weighed his options and looked around him. Charlie was a good time guy but he lived barely above street level. His mother and Herbert were a cause for shame. Sarah was living in a small house in Scottsboro, Alabama and barely had enough to eat. He was finished with riding the rails, punching cattle, and working as a whorehouse goon. On March the 7th, 1940, Paul walked into the recruiting office in Chattanooga and enlisted in the United States Army. It would be his home for nearly thirty years.

"Congratulations. You are now the lowest ranking private in the U.S. Army." The captain who swore him in had a grim look on his face and shook his hand. "Good luck, private. You'll need it." Paul's new status paid him twenty-one dollars a month, plus mess hall food, a bunk in a barracks, and standard-issue uniforms. All that, and the promise of adventure.

He was given a train ticket to Columbus, Georgia, where he and other arriving recruits were met by an Army bus and two screaming sergeants. The bus took them to Fort Benning for Basic Training. He was given uniforms, taught how to march and salute, and made to watch training films the purpose of which seemed to Paul to be the showing of disgusting footage of venereal disease and foot-rot to would-be soldiers who might one day find themselves so afflicted after a drunken round of sex or a few days in a wet foxhole. He was taught how to make his bunk, wear his hat, and mop the latrine.

One week into the training Paul contracted pneumonia and was hospitalized for a week. After one more week of training he was hospitalized for two weeks. The Army considered rejecting him as physically unfit but war was looming and the United States was building up its armed forces, so every man was needed. Upon his release from the hospital for the second time he was rushed through the rest of his training and sent to join the 16th Infantry on maneuvers in the swamps of Louisiana. The division was being readied for the war and its troop strength was growing with recruits like Paul, many of whom were Southerners who, as in previous wars, would prove to be outstanding fighters. In Louisiana he lived in the field for the first time, digging foxholes, pitching a pup tent, marching, attacking, defending, and pretending to shoot people. He found that he was a natural soldier.

Paul was surprised to learn that the 16th was temporarily based in New York City, on Governor's Island in the harbor. Ft. Jay was one of the oldest bases in the Army and dated to the Revolutionary War. He thought that was interesting in a way that a casual history buff would see it, but what grabbed his attention was the city itself. For a kid from the boondocks, recently of remote Western ranches and an Oregon whorehouse, New York City was paradise.

Soldiers were required to wear their uniforms while off base on pass and Paul wore his proudly, pressing his blouse and trousers, polishing his shoes and Sam Brown belt, and shining his brass. He felt like the King of New York as he stood in Times Square and gawked at the lights and the crowds, feeling the energy of the city. Taxis honked and sped by, street hustlers shouted enticements, pretty girls by the thousands walked by wearing fancy hats and high heel shoes. Anyone looking at Paul would see a country rube ripe for picking. Here was a kid who didn't know the score. So they thought.

"Hey, soldier, you want a girl?" The man who sidled up to Paul was short and had a bad leg. He had the eyes of someone who was deciding whether to buy a horse. He stared at Paul's face, waiting for the rube to respond.

"Who're you?" Paul asked, taking a step back.

"I'm a friend. I can, ah, arrange for some company, if you get my drift." The man moved closer and put his hand on Paul's arm.

Paul knew a hustler when he saw one. He had seen plenty on the trains and he recognized this man as someone who probably carried a blackjack or a knife. "No thanks."

"C'mon kid. She's beautiful. Redhead. You like redheads?"

"I said no thanks." Paul began to walk away.

The man was surprisingly fast for a gimp and he placed himself in front of Paul and the smile was gone. "Kid, you're gonna come with me. You won't regret it." He touched Paul again.

"Leave me alone or I'll call the police."

"Whatever you say, kid." The man smiled, tipped his hat, and disappeared into an alley.

Paul wondered what had just happened. He patted his pockets and found that his wallet was gone. He was out only a few dollars because he had been warned to leave most of his money in the barracks, but his Army identification and other personal items were lost, along with the kidskin wallet that had cost him ten dollars. He didn't have taxi fare back to the docks where an Army motor boat ferried the soldiers to and from the island, so he had to walk and missed the last boat. He spent the night on the dock and missed reveille in the morning. That cost him his pass into the city for thirty days. It also put him on KP, kitchen police, for a week, giving him plenty of time to consider the things he would do the hustler if he ever saw him again. He never did, but New York had no shortage of hustlers. In a sense, it was just a much bigger Chattanooga.

Manhattan was more than clubs and hustlers. A literate person of the era would have noticed that there were as many bookstores in Manhattan as there were bars. Paul wandered the city's neighborhoods and spent as much time browsing the book shelves as he did drinking with his friends. He read everything from history to pulp fiction to books about the way things work. He would spend an hour reading how to build a radio, then another hour reading a sordid mystery or cowboy story. He loved books about men who overcame the odds and triumphed, seeing himself as the heroes of these books.

A store in Greenwich Village had a back room where books of a certain kind could be found if the man behind the counter thought you were a customer and not a vice cop. This store had the usual fare in the front; high-brow novels, biographies of dead statesmen, literary publications and newspapers from other cities. There was a narrow hallway at the back that led to a curtained doorway through which a patron might pass to find literary works by authors such as D.H. Lawrence,

Henry Miller and Anais Nin that had the distinction of having been "banned" or, worse; cheap pulpy publications bearing large-breasted women on the cover and titles such as "Lust in the Dust."

Army barracks were prime markets for such books and Paul purchased them in bulk and re-sold them to his fellow soldiers for a healthy markup. He became a regular and got to know the man who ran it. He also made the acquaintance of an author of such books. The author's pen name was Jack Ram. The author's given name was Cecilia Delmonico. She worked outside the established publishing industry. She wrote her sordid tales on a bargain typewriter, using every perversion she had even heard rumored in scenes that brought laughs or howls from even the most jaded readers. She published them herself, using a printer who did not object to some off-the-books business, and she delivered them in person to bookstores known to carry such literary fare. She was a thirty-five year old Italian American from Brooklyn, brassy, foul-mouthed, a fine cook, and a woman with an eye for younger men who fit her standards of handsome. Paul fit the bill. He had movie star good looks, in her eyes, he was physically fit, and exotic in that he spoke with a thick Southern accent that she could barely understand.

"Who's the war hero?" she asked, shoving a pile of her latest book across the counter.

"Who knows? Who cares?" The counter man counted the books in the pile. "Fifty books at twenty cents. Your end is a sawbuck." He pushed a ten dollar bill across the counter.

"I'm only in it for the money," she said. "He come in here often?"

"What? You lookin' for story ideas? Yeah, he's a regular. Buys 'em by the stack and sells 'em to the guys in the barracks."

She walked over to Paul and looked him in the eye. "Hey, soldier boy, you like books?"

Paul was tongue tied. She had a direct stare that held him in place. "Yes, ma'am."

"Ma'am? You callin' me ma'am? Do I look like a fuckin' ma'am to you?" She had a smile on her face and a wink in her eye. "Ever meet a real author before? I write books, ya' know. I write these books, the ones you're sellin' to your soldier buddies."

"Yes, ma'am," he repeated. "I mean, okay."

"You look like you could use a good meal. It's on me."

It was the first such relationship for Paul, one that could be called "an affair." She lived in a brick building hidden behind a metal fire escape, four floors up, in a two room place that was cluttered with discarded sheets of paper that even she thought were too much for her readership. The place had a stained sink, an ice box, a two-burner gas stove, a few shelves, a cotton mattress over squeaky springs, and two wooden chairs. The rest was linoleum under scattered clothing, paper bags, magazines, and whatever she felt like tossing off the bed at odd moments.

Paul was still taking in the place and wondering how someone lived like that when she began to throw things onto the floor. "Hey, soldier. You look like you could use a nap. Funny thing. I got a bed here. Take a load off."

Over the course of the summer he spent at least one night a week in her place. She was an education for him in many ways. Her next potboiler had as its hero a Southern soldier whose daring do in the boudoir and on the battlefield would have made Napoleon blush.

When he wasn't with Cecelia he spent time in card and dice games where flotsam from the Armed Forces rubbed elbows with merchant seaman, local players, and anyone else with some cash and a willingness to put it in the pot.

His card playing skills learned on the ranches came in handy and his eye for cheats kept him up more than he was down. There was heavy drinking in the mix and tempers grew hot as regularly as the sun came up on the game in progress. There were times when the cash ran out and an item of value was placed in the pot. He lost his Bulova watch in one game and won a Longines time piece in another.

The games were played in backrooms and alleys, pool halls and private apartments. Sharpies who thought soldiers were easy marks hustled men in uniform into dark places and produced loaded dice or marked decks of cards. Only the freshest of hayseeds fell prey to these men. The soldiers, like Paul, had played a few hands of cards on their own.

Other men, some from the merchant ships tied up at the docks, were brought in to the games and thought that they, too, controlled the outcome.

Paul often found himself tipsy and in the company of hard men. A Portuguese seaman with a hot temper threatened to slice him open with a six inch, razor-sharp blade after the deal of one hand and lost his knife to Paul in the next. The knife stayed with Paul for the next forty years and he could never pick it up without saying to anyone nearby, "I won this off a Portuguese seaman in a card game in New York in 1940."

Chapter sixteen

The 4th of July that year was hot and muggy. The 16th Infantry's commander decided it was a great occasion to show off for the City of New York and so he ordered a parade. The unit's band was brought forth to provide the marching music as the soldiers trod across the parade ground, sweating and mumbling curses. They stood at attention as the general gave a speech that was forgotten as soon as the wind blew his words away. The troops then repaired to Manhattan watering holes to celebrate the birthday of America.

The fleet was in, meaning there were sailors flooding the same watering holes. The sailors called the soldiers "doggies" for dog face soldiers. The soldiers called the sailors "swabbies."

The trouble began in a place known by the name of the neon sign over the door. "Bar." It was the kind of bar where the pine plank floor was permanently stained with ancient beer and whiskey and scarred by long-ago fights. The chairs were bent cane with wicker bottoms that had holes from knives, broken glass, and the occasional fist.

The soldiers were lined up at the bar and gathered at a few tables, telling filthy jokes and complaining about the Army, when a half-dozen sailors walked in.

"Hey, check out the swabbies," said one of the soldiers.

The other men looked up. Most of them went back to what they were doing but a big soldier named Lamont stood up and put his fists on his hips. "This joint's for soldiers. You ain't welcome here. Go find your own bar."

Paul was feeling tipsy and trying to talk another soldier at the table into a dice game. He wasn't paying attention to the sailors.

One of the sailors went back out onto the sidewalk and whistled. That brought more sailors.

"Hey, doggie, go outside and piss on a fire hydrant," one of the sailors said. "This is now a Navy joint and we want you guys outta here."

That caught Paul's attention, along with all of the other soldiers. Some of them picked up chairs and held them over their heads. The bartender yelled for everyone to leave but his voice was drowned out by the insults being thrown back and forth and the sound of tables and chairs moving. There was no backing down in such moments when booze and manly pride overcame good sense.

Fists flew. Chairs were broken. Eyes were blackened. Blood seeped into the beer-soaked floor, and not for the first time. New York City and military police waded in and by dawn the next day, a Friday, the Manhattan House of Detention, widely known as The Tombs, the city's notorious jail, was filled with hung over servicemen nursing various cuts and bruises. One of them was Paul, who had a shiner and skinned knuckles.

The Tombs was at 125 White Street on a site originally used as a jail in the early Nineteenth Century, also called The Tombs. The "new" Tombs had been built in 1902. It contained individual cells and larger areas where drunks and other non-lethal street criminals were kept Paul and a mix of soldiers and sailors were locked up in a "tank", with a reeking toilet, rusty sink, and wooden benches along the walls.

"Hey, doggie, you got a fag?" The sailor was pale in his hangover but he tried to smile.

Paul reached into the breast pocket of his khaki shirt and offered his pack of Luckies. "Here. You look like hell."

"You're lookin' pretty good yourself, soldier boy." The man lit the smoke and took a deep drag.

Paul looked around at the men locked up with him and felt happy. His head hurt, his eye was swollen, he felt like throwing up, but he was happy in the company of these men, sailors and soldiers alike.

"Where'd you guys come in from?" he asked.

"We've been in the Pacific and came up through the canal. We got shore leave in Panama." The sailor smiled. "The ladies do it all down there."

"What's the Pacific like?"

"Depends. Hawaii is swarming with Navy and Army. They keep saying something big is gonna happen in the Pacific and they're building up the Navy like crazy. You ain't seen sailors 'til you been to Pearl Harbor."

"Hell, they're tellin' us to get ready for Europe." Paul was doing what soldiers and sailors have done since the beginning of time: swapping rumors. "We've been told to get ready for maneuvers that'll last for weeks, maybe months. There's lots of talk that we're shipping out soon."

"How long have you been in New York City?"

"I've been here a couple of months. It's just a holding area until we get a permanent base."

"What're the women like here?" It was another eternal question of soldiers and sailors.

"I don't have any complaints," Paul said, offering his best smile, bruised though it was.

"You boys put up a good fight," the sailor said.

"You boys ain't bad yourselves."

The Tombs was connected to the Manhattan Criminal Courts Building on Franklin Street by an elevated walkway known as The Bridge of Sighs. The fighters, Army and Navy, were marched across the bridge to a courtroom where a severe-looking elderly judge glared at them.

"You men are servants of the United States," he began. "I, for one, am disappointed that you would behave in such an unacceptable manner." The judge, in fact, had been a Doughboy during the Great War and knew full well how soldiers and sailors behaved in bars. "The city of New York does not condone, nor does it tolerate, hooliganism. Have I made myself clear?"

The men nodded and wore their most serious faces.

"Normally, I would issue a fine and send you on your way. However, I have received communications from your commanders. Men, I have some bad news." He looked up and smiled.

The Army commander of Ft. Jay and the admiral in charge of the sailors decided that, since it was a holiday weekend, The Tombs would be a fine place for the men to ponder the greatness of America's founding fathers. The soldiers and sailors were fully sober and properly repentant when they were released to their units on Sunday afternoon, having spent three nights as guests of New York City. But playtime was coming to an end. War was in the wind.

Chapter seventeen

President Franklin Roosevelt prepared the nation for war by asking Congress to authorize the nation's industry to begin the building of planes, tanks, weapons, and the other necessities of large scale conflict. *"We must increase production facilities for everything needed for the Army and Navy for national defense,"* he said. The President told Congress that America needed to build fifty-thousand planes, a two-ocean navy, and a much larger Army. The two-ocean navy was mostly a paper dream. The Army consisted of one hundred and eighty-seven thousand men. The Air Corp was laughable.

The 16th Infantry had no suitable base for training and even if it did there were no rifles, tanks, or cannons to use for training. The rifles Paul and his unit buddies trained with were wooden mockups. Small trucks were labeled "tanks" and were bombed with bags of flour because there were no real bombs to use. The Army of 1940 was barely above a Boy Scout troop. The War Department ordered a buildup and the Army went on permanent training status.

Paul received orders for the anti-tank company of the 304th Infantry Regiment and was sent to Edgewood Arsenal in Maryland for special training in landing maneuvers from ship to shore. In January of 1941 he boarded the U.S.S. Capella with a company of Marines and sailed to Guantanamo Bay, Cuba for a month of amphibious landings in which the Army attacked the Marines. He had never been to sea and spent the time vomiting over the side of either the U.S.S. Capella or the wooden landing craft that bobbed and jumped in the surf during the mock invasions.

In March the 304th was sent to Ft. Devens, Massachusetts to train for the expected war. For Paul, it would be a life-changing move, and not simply because of the Army training. In the fall of 1941 Paul was introduced to a French-Canadian woman named Marie. She lived in the small city of Lowell and worked in one of the textile mills along the Merrimack River. She was dark haired, dressed fashionably, spoke English with a French accent, and had a mind of her own. He was in love.

It was a strange courtship. He was a nominal protestant with a thick Southern accent. He had been around and knew a few things about life, even though he was several years younger than she. She had lived the sheltered life of a Catholic family where French was spoken, spiritual life was centered around St. Louis Parish, where everyone else spoke French, and had never been outside Massachusetts except for summer visits to nearby Hampton Beach, New Hampshire.

The truth was, they could barely understand each other. She took him to meet her family. Her father was appalled and refused to speak English in front of him. Her older brother Richard was a loudmouth who felt that anyone who was not French and was not raised in Lowell was a lesser being. Her sister Louise was flighty and flirty and had no interest in someone whom she considered an outsider. Her youngest brother Pete was the only one who tried to get to know Paul and convinced other family members to at least give him a chance.

Paul and Marie spent their weekends at dances and in the homes of friends. He mostly courted her on weekends following payday and spent every dime he had on her, hoping to impress her and her family. They talked into the night about the things that young people who are taken with each other talk about.

They exchanged letters following these weekends. One letter read:

I just received your letter and I sure was glad you wrote. I did not think you would write to me. You were pretty sleepy that night and I thought it would be our last until the first of the month. You know how I'm beginning to feel about you.

By December he was sure he wanted to marry her. Pete tried to explain it to Marie's father but the man was adamant. His French-Canadian Catholic daughter was not going to marry someone who seemed to be a foreigner who wasn't even Catholic. Besides, no one could understand a word he said. The man liked guns, for God's sake, and showed them off to everyone he met!

"No, Marie will find a good Frenchman who attends Mass, has a normal job, and wants to spend his life in Lowell," he said.

What the man didn't understand was that Marie had bigger dreams that went far beyond the confines of Middlesex County, Massachusetts. Whatever his faults, Paul was an adventurer and she wanted to go along. The adventure would last a lifetime.

Paul and Marie went for a drive on a clear, cold December Sunday. They had the radio on and were humming along with the Glen Miller orchestra when the announcer broke in.

"We interrupt this broadcast to bring you a special bulletin. The Japanese have bombed Pearl Harbor in Hawaii. Repeat, the Japanese have bombed Pearl Harbor in Hawaii. Stay tuned for more information as it becomes available."

Paul pulled the car into a rest area along the highway. He looked at Marie. They both knew that the world had changed.

"I have to get back," he said.

"I know," she replied.

He drove her home in silence and reported back to his unit, which had been placed on full alert. No orders were forthcoming, so life returned to something approaching normal at Ft. Devens while orders were prepared and the nation slipped into all-out war. For the lovers, time was precious. Paul and Marie were married in a civil ceremony on the 8th of January 1942 and broke the news to her father that night. Two days later they were married in a hastily arranged ceremony presided over by a Catholic priest. Marie's father would not speak to her for two years.

Paul was on leave for Christmas 1942 and the New Year's Eve that welcomed 1943. He and Marie celebrated in the way that young married couples do. Nine months later, Paul was on maneuvers in Florida when he received a telegram informing him that Marie had given birth to a son. He was given a five-day pass. Passenger trains were filled with soldiers, sailors and Marines who had priority over civilians. Even so, it took

Paul two days to reach Lowell and he was forced to stand the entire way. He spent one day with Marie and the boy, whom they named Paul Junior, before he boarded a southbound train and spent another two days standing on the trip back to his unit in Florida.

It was to be more than three years before Paul and Marie lived together. They joined millions of other couples whose lives were on hold as the Greatest Generation saved civilization.

Chapter eighteen

England in 1944 was the staging area for the largest invasion force the world had ever seen. For soldiers like Paul it was a grueling time of training. He lived in a squad tent with other soldiers, enduring days of bone-chilling cold as the men rehearsed beach landings, wading into the chilly waters off the coast of England over and over, storming across the sand, and doing it again. There weren't enough landing craft for the exercises, so mockups were used on the sands as the men lined up to learn their positions, how to get off in an orderly fashion and run across the beach.

Units were being created, broken up, and created again, as the generals configured their forces to attack the Germans in France. Paul had been shuffled around like a spare part, going to units that needed anti-tank gunners, training them, and moving on to another infantry company. He was a corporal now and was classified as a squad leader.

In early June the tension was high as the men sensed that, at last, the invasion was at hand. Paul was living in a muddy field and standing in line for a hot breakfast when word came down the line.

"Did you hear? The 101st and the 82nd jumped into France."

"Hey, did you hear? 1st and the 29th hit the beaches in France."

"Did you hear? The 4th and the 29th are in on it."

And so it went, rumors and unofficial reports, until General Eisenhower addressed his troops:

"Soldiers, Sailors and Airmen of the Allied Expeditionary Force! You are about to embark upon a great crusade toward which we have striven these many months. The eyes of the world are upon you. The hopes and prayers of liberty-loving people everywhere march with you. In company with our brave Allies and brothers in arms on other fronts, you will bring about the destruction of the German war machine, the elimination of Nazi tyranny over the oppressed peoples of Europe, and security for ourselves in a free world."

Paul listened in the company of other men who would soon be part of the great crusade and he wondered about the men who were hitting the beaches. Not one man believed it would be easy. Not one man was unafraid.

"How long before we go over?" The man asking the question was a soldier from New York.

"Could be any minute," Paul said. His knees were shaking and he hoped the others didn't notice. He sat on the wet ground and re-read letters from Marie. He wondered if he would ever see her again. He asked himself whether he would rather die than return to her as a cripple or a blind man. He knew the answer. He could never present himself as a lifelong burden to her.

The Americans still on English soil did not sleep that night. Their thoughts were with the men who were fighting and dying in Normandy. The air was filled with rumors. Omaha Beach was a blood bath, some said, and the Americans were driven back. Not so, said others, Germans were being killed by the thousands or had given up altogether. A soldier's life is dominated by three things: boredom, action, and rumors. Paul and his buddies had two out of three.

Three days later a master sergeant walked into Paul's tent and shouted, "Brite, Paul, Corporal!" and looked around.

"Here, Sergeant," Paul said, waving his hand.

"Grab your gear and report to company commander."

The captain was sitting at a field desk reading some papers when Paul reported and saluted. "Corporal, you've moving out. The 4th Division needs anti-tank gunners and you're been volunteered. There's a deuce and a half loading up. Be on it."

An hour later Paul was sitting in the back of an Army two-and-a-half-ton truck, rolling through the English countryside to a port where a small troop transport was being loaded to support the invasion, now inching inland from the beaches. The men climbed down from the truck and were met by load masters blowing whistles and shouting orders.

"You men, leave your duffel bags on the truck. You'll get new gear on the transport." A major walked up and the down the loading area, counting the replacements. "You'll get your duffel bags returned when you get back to England or they'll find you in France. If you have personal items you can't live without, now is the time to dig them out. No teddy bears or dirty pictures."

Paul had some of Marie's letters in his field jacket, so he left his duffel bag and joined the formation. The men were marched onto the transport, issued life preservers, and left on deck through the cold English night. The ship pulled into the English Chanel at dawn and the men were fed K-rations and lined up for new equipment, including packs and webbing, canteens, mess kits, M1 Garand rifles, a box of ammo, four hand grenades, and a bayonet with scabbard.

Paul went to a spot on the deck and found a seat. He assembled his field gear, cleaned his M1, and tried to keep from throwing up. Hours later, the transport stopped off Utah Beach and the men were loaded into landing craft. There were no sounds of fighting as the craft bobbed onto the beach and Paul stepped off into cold, knee-deep water and ran across the sand as he had been trained. Evidence of the fight was everywhere. Jeeps, artillery pieces, weapons and parts of uniforms were spread over the sand, next to the blood of the men who had died taking this bit of the French coast. The beach masters were screaming orders and waving the new arrivals to the dunes.

A company headquarters tent had been set up about a quarter mile from the beach and the replacements were ordered to report to the officer in charge of assignments. Hand-drawn signs had been stuck on wooden poles to direct the men to their proper areas. One sign read, "Anti tank gunners," and Paul walked over and got in line.

"Corporal Brite, you're moving out." The order came from a Sergeant First Class whose fatigues were filthy and torn. "There's your ride." He pointed to a truck set to tow a 57 millimeter M1 anti-tank gun. "Mount up, Corporal."

The 4th Division was in the process of linking up with the 101st Airborne Division inland from the beach and commanders were worried that German Panzers were going to break through the line and split the American units. Paul's anti-tank crew was dug in and waiting. The 57 was brought to a tree line and aimed at the German lines, ready to fire at the first Panzer units that came through the hedgerow. There was no sign of the Panzers. The German tanks were spread out and hiding from Allied aircraft, which were pounding the Germans and destroying much of their men and equipment.

Paul slept on the ground and ate K-rations. He could hear artillery shells in the distance and, now and then, small arms fire. A German probing patrol moved through the tree line under the protection of a lone Tiger tank. Paul allowed the tank to get within a hundred yards and opened fire. The first round bounced off the tank's front armor but it was enough to stop the Tiger and send the infantry near it to cover. The tank's turret moved as the German's looked for the source of the round. Paul's crew loaded and fired a second round, hitting the tank where the turret was attached to the body, sending up a plume of smoke and metal. The German tank crew jumped out and ran, carrying a man who appeared to be unconscious. The infantry with the tank pulled back.

Paul was ordered to move the anti-tank gun, an order that proved life-saving when the German 88s pounded the spot where Paul and his crew had been dug in. The Germans continued to probe along the American and British lines as the allies pushed them back. Over the course of the Battle of Normandy some two-hundred thousand German soldiers would be killed.

After two weeks on the line, Paul was sent back to England to rejoin the 304th. He was promoted to sergeant and made an assistant platoon sergeant. He spent his time regaling the men with stories of his time in France, which had been spent mostly waiting for something to happen.

England was damp and cold and the Christmas season was depressing. Paul wrote to Marie:

This English weather is getting me down. I don't like the damn place. I was in London and I don't like that, either. The only thing I liked was Westminster Abbey. I'm sending you the Christmas program. Honey, there isn't much to write about. Nothing is going on around here."

The 304th was enjoying its final quiet period of the war. While the unit was making its final preparations to join the battle against the Wehrmacht, the German high command had made the decision to make a final assault to split the Allied lines. In mid-December, the Germans attacked and the 'Battle of the Bulge' began. The Germans attacked along a broad front from the Ardennes forest in Belgium and into Luxemburg and France.

Paul's anti-tank company was packed up and ready to move out by the beginning of the New Year and for reasons only the Army could understand, spent six days crossing the English Chanel. The men of the 304th were ordered to organize their gear into horseshoe packs, complete with blankets, and head out on foot from Le Havre in a blinding snowstorm.

Paul was five-feet-ten and weighed one-hundred-forty pounds. He carried half his weight on his back. He was cold, wet, and his feet hurt. After ten miles of snow and ice, with stragglers struggling to keep up, Paul and his anti-tank company staggered into an open field. Paul fell to the ground, wrapped in his shelter half, and fell asleep, wet and cold.

A soldier next to him mumbled, "Welcome to France. Parlez vous?"

A small chorus of men picked up the tune, singing out into the snow, "Hinkey, Dinkey, Parlez Vous. Fuck you."

Life improved the next morning. Breakfast was Spam, white bread and coffee. Deuce-and-a-halfs appeared, engines running, and the anti-tank company was saved from another walk in the snow. That night Paul slept in a barn on a bed of hay and endured the cow that was in the next stall. Some of the men were suffering from frostbite and medics were doing what they could. A field kitchen offered hot meals.

Paul was on his way to the town of Beausaint, twelve miles from Bastogne. The Germans had broken through the Allied lines and had been stopped, but the battle was violently raging against the desperate Germans who were trying to keep the Americans from crossing into their homeland. German patrols were active around Beausaint and the 304th was told to be alert. Heavy fighting was ahead.

Paul and his 57 M1 team were positioned at the tree line of a large field that was covered in deep snow. The men wrapped themselves in anything they could find: blankets, newspapers, rags, scrap canvas from the trucks, extra uniforms. They were told to watch for men who wore American uniforms but formed up like

German infantry units. The Germans had been caught coming through the lines dressed as Americans.

The nights were bitterly cold and some Americans froze to death in their foxholes; others suffered frostbite so severe that they were no longer considered fit to fight. The Germans kept up their probes and the 304th discovered that the enemy came through the American lines at night and cut communications wires.

Paul was sent out to reconnoiter enemy lines and determine the position of the Panzers and other German armor. He saw many Panzers dug in but the crews were not visible. The 304th was ordered to move up and spent a hellacious night in blinding snow and ice with zero visibility moving a few miles. At dawn the regiment was spread back almost to its starting point with maintenance crews pulling jeeps, trucks and small armor out of ditches.

The weather warmed a bit and some of the snow melted. Hot chow was brought up. Letters from home arrived and Paul had a stack of them from Marie, all with gossip about her family and news that Paul Junior was getting bigger.

Paul wrote back:

"I wish I had a couple of those wool scarves of mine over here. It's colder than hell. There's a foot of snow on the ground and some of these hay barns we've been sleeping in are kind of drafty. Honey, this is slightly rugged. Don't worry about anything. I'll be all right over here. You just be all right over there.

All my love always,
Paul

The weather turned cold again and the anti-tank company moved up into the town of Mombach, where Paul's 57 M1 was positioned along a tree line near the road that led to the German lines. He went out to look for vulnerable spots where the German's might attempt to break through the 304th's lines. The Germans had other, more immediate plans.

The German 88's, one of the most feared weapons of the war, opened up on the town, raining its 88 millimeter shells on the Americans as they lined up for noon chow. At first the Americans thought the shells were being targeted to nearby American artillery pieces, but that opinion lasted only as long as it took for one of the shells to injure several of the 304th troops who were waiting to eat. The shelling continued well past dinner. Paul ran into a cellar and waited it out.

Paul was on the line, waiting for German armor to come up, but the German tanks remained where they were. The enemy was sending patrols behind the American lines to gather intelligence about the placement of artillery, anti-tank guns, headquarters, and other valuable information which would be used for the 88s targeting during daylight hours. The German patrols often hid among the Americans during the day.

Paul was awake and on watch just after midnight on a clear, cold night when he heard a voice. It was almost a whisper. There was only a sliver of a moon and the starlight did not offer a clear view. He was tempted to call out, "Who's there?" and issue a code word challenge, when he heard the voice again and saw what he believed to be several men hunched over and moving near the tree line.

"Dieses ist das siebenundfünfzig," the voice said.

"Ja," came a whispered reply.

Paul did not speak German but he knew what language he was hearing. He took his M1 off safety, aimed at a helmet that was visible, and fired. The helmet fell to the ground as the German patrol began yelling and firing back. Paul's men were awake in seconds and firing at the Germans in a firefight that lasted less than a minute. No American was hit but Paul became—in a way—the first American casualty of the anti-tank company. His canteen had been hit by a German round. The water in the canteen had frozen and was solid ice. The round had hit with such force that the canteen, attached to Paul's pistol belt along with ammo pouches, a medical kit, and a bayonet, had spun the belt and ripped some of the skin from Paul's hips. He was bleeding and laughing. The men were torn between congratulating him on his luck and commiserating about the missing skin.

The unit moved up again, this time up to the Sigfried Line, Germany's last defense of the homeland. On the other side of the Sauer River lay Germany itself and victory.

Chapter nineteen

The German high command had placed a monumental bet on the attack that was to be known as the Battle of the Bulge and it had failed. The Americans had fought back and closed the gap and were now at the very doors of the homeland. German orders were given to stop them from crossing the Sauer. The American command sent an order to the 304th: cross at all cost. The regiment was part of a massive American force arrayed along what Hitler called The Western Wall. Many of these American units had suffered terrible losses in the Battle of the Bulge and the men and their commanders were determined to make the Germans pay.

Tuesday, February 6th, men of the 304th prepared to support their engineers, who were going to place a foot bridge across the river to allow the unit to grab and hold ground until a larger bridge could be put in place to bring heavy weapons across. The 304th historian would later write that there was so much artillery going back and forth that it seemed to stop in mid air and roar.

Just after midnight on the 7[th,] boats were loaded and men and machine guns began moving into Germany. Paul's anti-tank gun was aimed at the German side and was set to fire at any threat to the men who were jumping from the boats and heading for high ground. The German lines were protected by pillboxes and entrenchments and the Americans took murderous fire as they moved through. Engineers used smoke grenades to hide their work. Artillery spotter planes flew at suicidal altitudes to drop supplies and ammunition. The engineers worked like dogs to build the bridge while the German's rained fire down on them.

Paul's anti-tank 57 M1 team was ordered to cross the bridge as soon as the engineers were ready. Before dawn he and his crew were in Germany, exchanging fire with German tanks manned by men who were now fighting on their own land. Paul's team and the rest of the 304th poured all they had into the Germans, knocking out tanks and other armor, moving into Germany.

At dawn the German town of Echternach was in American hands and the engineers had completed a heavy equipment bridge. The battalion commander called it a "no man's land" and told his men to listen for the sounds of the German 88s. The big shells came in all day and Paul and the other soldiers huddled in whatever shelter they could find. Other men in the 304th were not so fortunate.

The Americans may have moved into Germany but the soldiers of the Reich were far from beaten. They were still in many of the pillboxes and Americans were killed by German machine guns and mines. Paul's anti-tank crew was busy trying to knock out anything the 57s could hit. Paul was cold, wet, and exhausted but there was no break in the fighting. Both sides suffered casualties and German prisoners were becoming a problem. They had to be sent to the rear but every man was needed for the combat that was underway.

After days of bitter fighting, two German officers approached the American lines under a white flag. They said they were occupying a town behind their own lines that was being used exclusively as an evacuation center for their sick and wounded. They asked that the town be declared an "open city" long enough to get their men out. They offered assurances that the period would not be used to build their forces for an attack. American commanders kept them overnight and granted the request, along with a two-hour cease fire so the wounded could be removed from the battle area.

The Sigfried Line had been breached but not eliminated. Men died from the fire coming from the pillboxes. American engineers died trying to blow them up. Paul's anti tank gun and other heavy weapons continued to pour fire at them.

More bridges were built to allow allied forces to build up their troop strength and supplies for the drive into Germany. Paul's unit was in place for a month, skirmishing and firing, taking prisoners, taking casualties, and killing Germans.

The 304th was ordered to move north to Holsthum, east to Alsdorf and Mackel, then south to Helensburg and Olk. The movement, in concert with other units, would encircle the remaining Germans north of the Sauer. It would require another river crossing, this one at Holsthrum where the 304th's engineers would build \bridges across the Prun, a small picturesque river in a serene setting, at least in peacetime. The Germans had no intention of making it easy.

The unit moved north and word came that—once engineers had erected the bridge—infantry, anti tank, and tank-killer companies would be given priority to cross the river and seize and hold ground. Paul gathered with other men as an officer read a message from the regimental commander:

"It must be successful. I know you and your men are capable. Good luck to you."

The Prum would be crossed at two spots: one to the north of Holsthrum, one to the south. The men were told to shed all unnecessary equipment. They received extra rations and ammunition. Paul's anti-tank crew made ready and moved out with the infantry on the evening of February 24th just before midnight. The engineers had put a small bridge across the Prun and Paul and the others crossed under German fire that was light and ineffective. The other side of the river was hilly ground that was heavily wooded and he his crew struggled to get the anti-tank gun and its ammunition to higher ground.

At daybreak German snipers began firing into the Americans and two were hit. The 304th troops came to an open field and the unit's heavy weapons were brought up to provide support for the infantry that would cross. Paul's 57 was at the tree line when all hell broke loose. The Germans opened up with small arms and machinegun fire backed by mortars. There was a small barn in the center of the field and the American infantry made for it, finding shelter.

Paul's 57 joined other heavy weapons and blasted the German positions, knocking out machineguns and mortars in a furious fight that caused heavy casualties among the Germans. One of the American platoons was left with only five able men at the end of the battle. Paul's anti-tank crew was mentioned in the after action report, along with medics and communications troops who had fought off the Germans. It was pointed out that the anti-tank unit had fought as infantry during the fight and had even ferried ammunition to the riflemen.

Paul spent the night reliving the battle and trying to calm his nerves. His friends noticed that his ready smile was gone and he no longer told jokes. His cheery goofiness had been replaced by a hard stare. He stayed to himself.

American units up and down the line were facing heavy German resistance. Other divisions, some bloodied by the Battle of the Bulge, were struggling to overcome the Wehrmacht's determined defense. Both sides were suffering casualties but the Americans were steadily advancing in bitter winter weather.

German civilians were sullen as the Americans moved through their towns. The people of France, Belgium and Luxembourg had welcomed the Yankees as liberators. The German people saw them as conquerors.

Paul had grown used to the sight of dead German soldiers on the roads and in the fields, lying near dead cows and horses and wrecked wagons and trucks. The people of Belgium had spit on the German corpses or kicked them. But to the German civilians, the dead were their sons and husbands. The German civilians were not eager to supply intelligence to the American units about the placement of German soldiers. Snipers were a problem. They were being sheltered by the people. Nearly every German village had Wehrmacht soldiers dressed in civilian clothing to avoid capture by the Americans.

Paul and the others grew wary of everyone they saw. They approached each house with caution, even those where the occupants were smiling and waving. Too often these gestures were traps to lure the Americans within range of snipers.

The Germans sent recon teams behind the American lines to spot artillery positions, headquarters tents, marshaling areas and fuel depots. Paul was assigned to guard one of the fueling areas on a cold, cloudy afternoon. He was carrying an M1 Garand and several clips of ammo, walking the perimeter, composing a letter to Marie, when he saw movement on the far side of the fuel depot. A man was running from the tree line to the makeshift fence that surrounded the tankers, drums, and five gallon cans that held the fuel that moved the unit.

The man disappeared behind a tanker and Paul ran to see where he was and identify him. Paul found him between two fully-loaded gasoline tankers. The intruder was a German soldier carrying two canvas bags and a rifle. Paul raised his M1 and ordered the man to surrender. The German laughed and pointed to his rifle and the tankers.

"Boom!" he shouted and ran into a thicket of five gallon cans that were also filled with fuel.

Each time Paul caught him within rifle distance the man either pointed to the tankers and ran, or he was too close to a fuel tank and Paul could not fire without risking a conflagration. Paul chased him and shouted "Halt!" without effect.

The German made it to the center of the depot and opened his bags, exposing TNT and detonators that he prepared to set in his mission to blow up the fuel. Paul saw him through a line of tankers and determined that he had narrow corridor behind the German that was clear of fuel containers. The German didn't notice Paul kneeling and aiming the M1. The man looked up as Paul fired, hitting the German in the chest. The shot brought other soldiers into the fuel area and the German was taken to a medical tent where he was treated. The man survived and ended the war in a camp in France.

Paul's company commander called him to the CP and Paul expected that he would be commended for saving the fuel. Instead, he was dressed down. "You damn fool. You could have blown us to hell. The Kraut didn't fire. That should have told you something. Now report back to your crew."

Paul stomped back to his gun muttering, "I'm not the damn fool around here."

Chapter twenty

The American line advanced into heavy combat day by day, with the Germans giving ground only after determined American assaults. Paul and his crew were moved up and down the line as commanders called for anti tank units to deal with Panzers and other German armor that was attacking the line. The 88s rained their big shells on American positions and took a brutal toll on the men who were moving up. One area near Helenenberg was dubbed Purple Heart Corner, another Bloody Hill.

Paul was exhausted and numb to the carnage. He moved through villages that had been reduced to a few standing stone walls, the streets littered with dead Germans and horses. His 57 fired into German tanks, half-tracks, machinegun nests, and anything else that threatened the American troops. He rode in the passenger seat of the truck that pulled the gun and had no emotion as he felt the bumps when the truck drove over a body. His world was the war and the nightmare went on and on. He pulled into the town of Helenenberg where the rumor had it that hot chow was available and saw a line of litter bearers outside what had been an orphanage. Inside, dead and wounded Americans were lined up and being cared for by exhausted medics and Army doctors. He thought of a scene from 'Gone With The Wind' and idly pondered the idea that nothing really changes.

He stood in line with his mess kit, waiting for something that looked like stew, and acknowledged that he was only feet from a place where men like him were dying. He was alive and they were dead. *War is people dying, he* thought, *and all the politics in the world doesn't change that.* He accepted that he, too, might soon be among the dead or the crippled. He quietly vowed to shoot himself rather than return to Marie as less than a whole man.

He sat on what remained of a stone wall and ate the hot food without tasting it. It was fuel, nothing more. He cleaned his mess kit in a drum of hot water, shook it dry, and folded it up to place it in his pack. He hadn't changed his clothes in days and allowed himself a fantasy of a hot shower and clean clothing. He sat down and changed his socks, one of the basic elements of field hygiene that could be the difference between trench foot and the ability to walk. He hung his dirty socks on his pack to dry and walked to the company command post where the First Sergeant was leaning over a map.

"Ah, Brite. Just the man I want to see." The First Sergeant, known as "First Shirt," needed a shave and a bath. His uniform was torn and his boots were wet.

"Hello, First Sergeant," Paul said. "You look like you could use some boots."

"Boots and bottle of Canadian Club. Ain't neither available just now. 4th Division's run into some trouble and needs some AT crews to help them out." He pointed to a spot on the map. "Their CP's right here. You chow down yet?"

"Yes."

"Get your crew and move out."

The 4th was no different than any of the other American units along the line as the Germans fell back in the following weeks. Attack, defend, attack. Cold, exhaustion, hunger, death. The snow melted and the earth turned to mud. American units were slowed by the knee-deep mud on the makeshift roads and even tanks got stuck. The only consolation was that the Germans were also bogged down in it.

Paul's clothes became stiff with dried mud and sweat and his boots began to rot. The 57 fired at the retreating Germans, along with everything else the Americans could throw at them. Leaves appeared on the trees and even flowers made an appearance in the forests of Bavaria. During lulls in the fighting Paul and the other men idled in the sun and admired the beautiful countryside.

"What do you think this place is like when people ain't shooting at each other?" he asked.

"Pretty nice, I'd imagine," his assistant platoon sergeant said. "Probably lots of pretty frauleins lookin' for a good time."

"Ain't nobody havin' a good time these days," Paul replied.

"Well, it's almost over," the sergeant said.

"Almost ain't good enough," Paul said. "There's lots of fightin' left, I think."

The April sunshine helped to dry out the men and equipment and the Germans continued to fall back. There was almost a lightness among the American soldiers of the 4th Infantry Division. That lightness turned to darkness on April 29th near the Bavarian town of Dachau.

Word had come back to the men that a concentration camp had been discovered there and the Red Cross was trying to negotiate a surrender. Paul was with the units that approached the camp and saw guards in the towers. Paul looked through the barbed wire fences and saw stacks of bodies wearing striped clothing. Emaciated human beings were staggering over bare ground and falling onto the piles of the dead.

He stood at the main gate, which was closed, and read the legend *Arbeit macht frei.* Late in the afternoon of the 29th, the SS commander of Dachau surrendered to the Americans and the gate was opened. Paul walked through the gate and into the camp and threw up. Other Americans did the same. Some fainted. Paul had a small camera and film which he used to take photos of the war, always shooting away from horrible images and taking pictures of the men he served with or villages that were still standing. Not so at Dachau. He walked to the piles of the dead and snapped photo after photo, afraid that no one would believe what he was seeing.

The SS guards were still in the towers, where white sheets of surrender were displayed. The guards smiled and waved at the Americans and asked for cigarettes. What happened next would be the subject of reports and investigations for years after the war ended. What is known is that at the end of the day every SS guard at Dachau was dead at the hands of the Americans. One Army report put the number at fifty; another at "only thirty." In the late 1940s, an Army report would claim the number was over five hundred. At the time, General Dwight Eisenhower stated that, "three hundred SS camp guards were quickly neutralized."

The Americans liberated thirty-two thousand human beings that day. And stuffed into his pack as a reminder of the worst thing he had ever seen or ever would see, Paul carried the Nazi flag that had hung over Dachau. He would keep it locked in a metal footlocker for the rest of his life as testament to the evil humanity is capable of and a tribute to the rage that can exact revenge. He would never experience one minute of remorse over his actions on April 29th, 1945.

Chapter twenty-one

The war ended in May. Hitler was dead. Europe was in ruins. Millions were homeless and destitute. But the hostilities were not over. Germany had surrendered but the Nazis had created a cadre of fanatical young men known as Hitler Youth who had gathered in secret cells to pursue their hatred of everyone who was not an Aryan German. They were armed, dangerous, and looking for Americans to kill.

Paul was sent to a holding camp where Americans were being processed for movement back to the United States according to their "points", meaning how long they had been in combat. Priority went to the men who had landed on D-Day and been on the line ever since, nearly a year of constant combat. Paul's points didn't allow him to be among the first to go home and he was assigned to a unit that was rounding up Hitler Youth.

He was a platoon sergeant and was in charge of a team that was given a two-and-a-half-ton truck and a map showing the location of a group of young men who were terrorizing German civilians and warning them against cooperating with the Americans. The young men had killed a man and his wife for accepting hot food from the Americans. The reality that no other food was available was not relevant to the Hitler Youth, who told the civilians that it was preferable to starve to death than take anything from the Yankee *sweinhunts*, or pig dogs.

Frankfurt was in ruins. Old buildings that had stood for centuries were now piles of stones and broken furniture. The main streets had been cleared by Army bulldozers that had pushed the rubble up onto what had been sidewalks. People were living in rooms that had no walls or roofs. The civilians in Frankfurt considered themselves fortunate that they were not under Soviet control to the east, where Russian soldiers were raping every woman they found and shooting every man that came within the range of their firearms. Still, life was hard and food was scarce. Some people were surviving on the garbage the Americans left behind their mess halls.

Paul and his men had no trouble finding the Hitler Youth. They had tied a sheet to a still-standing storefront proclaiming *Deutschland ist frei,* Germany is free. The Americans climbed down from the truck and spread out in a squad formation. The young German men walked out of the building with smirks on their faces and Nazi arm bands on their shirts, issuing a Hitler salute and shouting, "Heil Hitler!"

Paul had learned a few German phrases. He aimed his M1 at the young man who appeared to be the leader and shouted, *"Übergeben Sie Ihre Waffen."* Surrender your weapons.

"Sie sind Schweine!" You are pigs.

"Übergeben Sie Ihre Waffen jetzt." Surrender your weapons now.

The young men appeared to hesitate and Paul knew that they were making up their minds whether to fight or give up. He aimed over the head of the leader and fired a warning shot. The other Americans also fired and moved on the men. Within seconds the combat veterans had the situation under control and were moving the Hitler Youth to the truck. Each young man was searched and ordered to climb up. The young man who was the leader of the group jumped up on the bed of the truck without waiting, pulled out a Luger, and aimed it at Paul's chest. An American soldier standing on the truck knocked the German's arm down as he fired. The bullet ricocheted off the ground and lodged just below Paul's left knee.

Paul and the young man looked at each other, the German with a smile on his face and Paul in pain. Paul knelt on his good knee, aimed the M1, and shot the German in the face.

The American who had saved his life handed Paul the Luger. "Here, he doesn't need it anymore." The Luger would find its place next to the Nazi flag from Dachau.

The summer of 1945 was a period of waiting to go home. Discipline was a problem for American commanders. Combat-hardened troops who had nothing to do were hard to control. Some of the men had heard that the Russians were using German women in any way they wanted and went on rampages on their own. Some of the men believed that they were conquerors and were entitled to whatever they saw; woman, silver, wine.

Paul was pressed into military police duty; knocking heads and ferrying drunken soldiers back to camp or to the stockade where they would await court martial. He was bored, anxious, and eager to get home to Marie and Paul Junior, who had been nicknamed "Buddy" to avoid calling him "Junior."

He was a different man from the one who sailed off to Europe and the war. He rarely smiled. He found solace in drink. He could not sleep. He became known as "a hard-ass NCO" among the troops who were under him and he was not afraid of a fist fight. He had disarmed several men who came after him with knives, knocking them unconscious with the butt of his M1. He did not know how he would live as a normal person with a wife and son. He didn't know what normal was. He was aware that he had never spent a normal minute in his life, at least normal as others would define it.

He boarded a troop ship at Bremerhaven in early December of 1945 for the trip home. It was an eighteen-day voyage on an aging vessel that had spent the war ferrying goods and supplies to the Soviet Union and was on its way to the scrapheap. He lived below decks in a cargo area that had been strung with hammocks. There were no latrines, only fifty gallon drums that had been cut in half. One of the details assigned to the men who were discipline problems was tossing the contents over the side twice a day. The showers were seawater and cold. The hold where Paul spent the voyage smelled like dirty men and latrine effluent. Fights were common. Paul was involved in as many as he broke up.

Finally, the ship chugged into New York Harbor, past the Statue of Liberty, to a berth in Brooklyn. The men lined up, hoisted their duffel bags onto their shoulders, and walked onto American soil after winning the war in Europe. A casual observer would have been hard pressed to find a smile. The men coming off the ship would go back to their lives and in coming decades build the most prosperous nation the world had ever seen. They would be doctors, lawyers, business owners, scientists and teachers. They would live in new suburban houses and their children would be called Baby Boomers. But at that moment, they were tired and they had seen the worst of human history.

Some of those who came back would not be part of the great prosperity. They would be the ones who carried on the fight, in their own way, to look after America's interests, good and bad. For them, there would be no peace and no rest from conflict. Paul was one of these men, although he had no way of knowing that as he took a bus to Grand Central Station and a train to Lowell.

Chapter twenty-two

Lowell, Massachusetts was on its way down in the mid '40s. Its "mile of mills" along the Merrimack River was reduced to a few open mills and others that were falling down, victim to the textile industry's new interest in states like North Carolina, where labor laws were friendlier to business owners. But Lowell, Lawrence and the other old mill towns were still the major employers and generators of the local economy and there were jobs to be had for the returning servicemen.

Paul had promised Marie that he would try to live a normal life. To her, that meant a steady job in one place. He had never had what in Marie's family would be described as a "job." He had been a hobo, a cowboy, a whorehouse bouncer, and a soldier. The whorehouse was the only place where he'd worked indoors. He did not have a high school diploma. He did not have any skills not related to firearms, horse riding, or fisticuffs.

Paul suffered from the effects of the war. He could not sleep. He was often in a foul mood and snapped at anyone nearby. He drank too much. He hated Lowell and everyone who lived there with the exception of Marie and Buddy. He found the people to be closed-minded and provincial. Most of them hated everyone who was not what they were. The French Canadians hated the Irish and the Italians, who hated them and each other. A French-Canadian Catholic marrying an Irish

Catholic was called a "mixed marriage," followed by the words, "They never work."

He was Southern and had no religion in a traditional sense. The war had convinced him that God didn't exist. If He had, Paul reasoned, He would never have allowed Dachau and the other camps and all of the suffering that swept the world during those years. Yet Paul was pressured to attend Mass with Marie, Buddy, and her family. He agreed to meet with a priest to discuss converting to the Church. Nothing the priest said touched him in a spiritual way. He felt, but never expressed it out loud, that the ceremony, the Latin, the incense and all the rest of it were just so much silliness and show.

He found a job at a factory that made shoes and was assigned to the night shift as a loader, a man who stacked boxes of shoes onto pallets for shipment. His boss was a fat, pasty Irishman who had avoided the war by claiming the making of shoes was critical to national defense. He teased Paul about his accent and liked to tell him about how easy the women were with their men gone.

"I'd watch that little Frenchie you got," he said, with a leer in his eye.

"I'd watch my mouth if I was you," Paul said, feeling humiliated.

"You're forgettin' somethin', friend," the man answer. "You work for me. I can change that right now."

Paul went back to stacking boxes.

His home life was tense. Marie was working in a textile mill operating a sewing machine from seven in the morning until three in the afternoon. Paul was left to watch Buddy, who was three and a handful. Buddy didn't really know Paul and was afraid of him. He assumed that Paul's anger was because he had done something wrong, but he didn't know what it was.

Paul began to drink during the day while Marie was at work and he was sullen and withdrawn when Marie got home, tired, hungry and ready to relax. They were together for less than an hour before Paul went to his job and it was unpleasant for both of them.

"Do you have to drink all day?" she asked. "How can you look after Buddy in that condition?"

"I can look after him just fine," he said, putting on a fake smile. "He ain't much of a bother."

"You can't look after a three year old if you're drunk. You need to get some help, Paul."

"How do you propose that I get help and where do you think I should go? To the priest? What's he gonna do, tell me to say my prayers?"

"The Army has people who take care of these things. It's been in the papers. You can go see them in Boston and just tell them what's going on with you. Please, do it for me. Me and Buddy."

It took a month for Paul to agree to see an Army psychiatrist at a center in Boston and another month for him to get an appointment. Paul arrived on a Tuesday morning at ten and saw a dozen men sitting in standard-issue chairs in a hallway outside the office of an Army major. Every man looked the same; somber, miserable, angry, and beaten. It was midafternoon before Paul was called into the major's office. Sitting behind a government desk was a middle-aged man wearing an officer's uniform, a bushy mustache, and serious expression on his face. The man had a smoking pipe sticking out of his mouth. He waved Paul to a chair in front of the desk.

"Name?" he said."Say it like you would to an officer when you were on active duty."

"Staff Sergeant Paul Brite, sir."

"What was your assignment, Sergeant?"

"Platoon sergeant in an anti-tank company, sir."

"See much combat?"

"Yes, sir."

"What's the problem?"

Paul spent the next thirty minutes telling the major more than he had ever shared with another man. He talked about the Battle of the Bulge, fighting into Germany, and the liberation of Dachau. He explained how humiliated he felt every night at his job and how helpless he was to do anything about it. He explained that he was not able to be much of a husband and, in fact, he and Marie didn't really know each other because they had been separated by the war.

"Did you notice the name on the little sign in front of my desk?" the major asked.

Paul looked at. It read: D. Steinberg, M.D.

"My name is Steinberg, sergeant. I'm Jewish. I'll be honest with you. I'm honored to meet a man who liberated Dachau. I don't care what happened to the SS guards." He stared at Paul and looked up at the ceiling. "Wait! I do care. Thank God they're dead. That's point number one. Point number two is this: I believe you belong back in the Army and I'm not saying that just because they're looking for NCOs with combat experience now that we seem to have a problem with the Soviets. In my professional opinion, you don't belong in a shoe factory in Lowell. If you stay there your marriage won't last and, frankly, neither will you." He sat back and puffed on his pipe, waiting for Paul to react.

"What do I tell Marie?"

"Tell her whatever you like but be honest."

French-Canadian women can be volatile. A Latin streak runs in their veins and they are not inclined to suffer in silence. Marie let him have it.

"The Army? What the hell is wrong with you? That war is over! You have a wife and child you need to support. You can't support a family on Army pay. Do you expect me and Buddy to follow you from camp to camp?" She slumped at the kitchen table and looked disgusted. "If you go, you go by yourself."

Paul went to the bedroom and packed a small suitcase. He walked out without saying goodbye and took a bus to the train station, where he bought a ticket to Boston. The Army recruiter was happy to see a combat veteran walk in the door and signed him up at his old rank. It would be a year before Marie heard from him. In that time she struggled as a single mother whose husband had left her. She worked at the textile mill and paid an elderly Greek woman to look after Buddy.

Her father reminded her that "outsiders who aren't French" can't be trusted. "Was I right or was I right?"

In 1947 a letter arrived from an Army Post Office address. She recognized the handwriting.

Chapter twenty-three

The First Cavalry Division was on duty in Japan. It was a proud unit whose history began in west Texas where the mounted troopers chased bandits and renegade Indians. The division has the largest patch in the Army, at five-and-a-quarter inches high. One legend has it that the division needed a patch large enough to be seen from horseback in the west Texas dust. The patch is a Norman shield with a yellow background and a black horses head over a black diagonal stripe. The division had fought in the Pacific and drew duty in Japan as part of the occupation force.

Paul was a platoon sergeant in a reconnaissance company. In truth, there wasn't much for him to do. The platoon trained one week a month and spent the rest of its time listening to hygiene lectures or cleaning and re-cleaning its weapons. There were lectures on Japanese culture and dangers of having sex with local prostitutes. Most of the soldiers in the platoon had entered the Army near the end of the war or after hostilities had ceased, so they had not seen combat. They wanted Paul and the other combat vets to tell them gory stories of gunning down Nazis or Japs, but those who had seen the fighting had no stomach for story-telling.

The unit was assigned to barracks on the outskirts of Tokyo and NCOs had permanent passes to leave the base and see the sights. Paul was restless and he felt guilty about leaving Marie and Buddy. It took him months to work up the courage to send a letter.

Hello Honey.

I am sorry about how things were left. I am back in the Army and stationed in Japan. I would like to get back together. I miss you and Buddy. Please think about joining me here. The Army will take care of everything and even provide a house for us.

All my love,
Paul

A month later he received a letter that broke his heart.

You hurt me and you left your son without a father. I don't know what I feel about you but I think it's time you got to know your son. Our job is to look out for him now. We'll see what happens with you and me.

The Army was trying to make life easier for its troops and had in place a program under which dependents could join their service member in locations considered safe for American civilians. Japan was seen as a safe place and the U.S. Military began to build housing for the families of members of the Army, Navy, Air Force and Marines.

It would be months before Marie and Buddy made the journey. The housing for dependents was still being built. Paul was anxious and bored. He needed an outlet for his energy and he found it at the Kodokan, the worldwide center of judo. The war had nearly brought the sport to a stop but the post-war period was a time of revival as Japanese men sought solace and pride in the art of "the gentle way."

Most of the students at the Kodokan were Japanese men, some of whom had fought against the Americans in the war. They were not eager to train Americans in the finer points of judo and they did not welcome Paul. But he was, after all, one of the conquerors and could not be turned away, so he enrolled in an intensive program that had him on the mat five nights a week for three hours. The Japanese discovered that the American was tough and could take punishment, which they dished out under the guise of "training."

It began with a week of learning how to fall, first as a drill on his own, then from throws administered by his sensei, a tiny, elderly man with white hair, few teeth, who stood about five feet tall. To an observer the sensei, or teacher, appeared frail and a street thug would see him as an easy mark for a robbery or worse. But the man was a roku-dan, a sixth-degree judo master who wore a red and white belt. For him, it meant that the frail old man who wore no expression on his face could throw Paul around the mat like he was a small child. Paul had no sensation of being thrown. One minute he was standing and facing his sensei and the next he was on his back. The other students tried to hide their delight.

A young Japanese man who appeared to be around Paul's age was assigned as his partner in the nightly drills to learn and master the throws, pins, chokes, and arm locks. The man did nothing to hide his distaste for Paul and went out of his way to inflict pain and discomfort. Paul found it liberating, freeing his own aggression, and the two men stopped just short of murder in their nightly contests on the mat. He came away with bruises and aches but he felt exhilarated. He drank less and grew stronger and clear-eyed. He began to understand that judo is, at its center, about balance, not strength, and that understanding spilled over into other areas of his life, helping him heal from the war.

He signed up for education classes and finished high school. He enrolled in a new program from the University of Maryland to offer courses to military personnel, taking English and history courses. He realized for the first time in his life that he was smart and learned easily.

He grew to appreciate the discipline of judo and the mental toughness that was required to master it. He had a natural ability to fight and warrior's desire to triumph and after a year of five-nights-a-week practice and matches, he was called to the front of the students and awarded a black belt. The Japanese applauded and bowed. Even his longtime foe on the mat applauded and smiled. He was as happy as he had been since before the war.

In March of 1948, Marie and Buddy joined hundreds of other dependents at a pier in Brooklyn and boarded the USS Alexander, an aging luxury liner that had been pressed into service as a transport during the war. The Military Sea Transport Service, known as MSTS, was now in the business of hauling women and children to faraway places. The luxury of the Alexander was a distant memory as the vessel set out past the Statue of Liberty and headed south to the Panama Canal and across the Pacific to Yokohama on a thirty-day journey of bad food, screaming children, resentful women, and a crew that couldn't wait to drop off their passengers.

On a glorious April day, the Alexander pulled up to a pier in Yokohama and hundreds of Americans who had never been very far from their birthplaces walked down the gangways and onto Japanese soil to the waiting arms of soldiers, sailors, airmen and Marines.

Paul was wearing pressed khakis and had flowers in one hand and a stuffed toy in the other. He was as nervous as he had ever been. Marie and Buddy were assaulted by smells, sights, and people they had never experienced. The dock workers wore only loin clothes and headbands. Yokohama smelled of fish and diesel fuel.

The procession of American soldiers, wives and children was led to busses that took them to their new homes. Grant Heights was a brand new housing area for American dependents in Tokyo. It was laid out like an Army base, which it was. Two and three-bedroom row houses arranged in quadrangles with an open space in the center, much like parade grounds.

Paul, Marie and Buddy were assigned to a two-bedroom end unit near rice paddies that were farmed by local men and women. Human excrement was used as fertilizer, giving the neighborhood an odor that Marie never got used to.

And so, for the first time, the Brites settled in as a military family overseas. The Japanese government, as part of its war reparations, was required to provide servants to the Americans. The Brites had a houseboy and a maid for their little row house. Paul and Marie made friends with the others in the occupation force.

They visited Mount Fuji, soaked in hot springs, bought souvenirs, and walked the narrow streets.

Life was sweet for Paul and Marie. They fell in love again. The sweetness ended on June 25, 1950. Soviet-backed North Korean troops crossed the 38th parallel into U.S.-supported South Korea. The cold war had turned hot. The 1st Cavalry Division was placed on war alert. Dependents were to be sent home. Paul arranged a transfer back to Ft. Devens so he could escort his family back to Massachusetts. Later, he would be sent to Korea to fight again.

The 1950's

Chapter twenty-four

Victory is reserved for those who are willing to pay its price.
Sun Tzu

Shortly after midnight in the chilly autumn of 1950, Paul drove his 1946 Hudson from Lowell to Ft. Devens. Marie was sitting beside him, wiping her eyes and trying to maintain her composure, and Buddy was sleeping in the back seat. An MP at the gate stopped the vehicle, Paul displayed his military ID, and the car was waved through. He drove to area of two-story wooden barracks that had been erected as "temporary" buildings during World War One and parked the car next to several others that contained families saying goodbye.

Paul was wearing fatigues and he went to the trunk of the Hudson and opened it. He removed his combat gear: helmet and liner, webbing, pack, shelter half, blanket, pistol belt, canteen, ammo pouches, and the rest of it, all assembled. He wouldn't need it for several weeks, but the Army had decried that soldiers being sent to Korea bring their gear with them, given that the situation on the peninsula was deteriorating and supplies were uncertain. The South Korean capital of Seoul had been captured by the communists for the second time. American commanders were planning an all-out offensive.

Paul had been re-assigned to the 1st Cav's recon company. He had no illusions about where he was going or what he would be doing. He tried to hide it from Marie but she knew that he was tense. He had become moody again and had trouble sleeping, which caused him to drink too much. An old pattern had resurfaced in their marriage.

He grabbed his gear and leaned into the car. "Bye, Baby. You take care of yourself and that boy." He opened the back door and kissed Buddy, who woke up in time to see his father disappear into a crowd of other soldiers. Buddy lay awake on the drive back to Lowell, listening to his mother crying.

Paul spent the next three weeks on trains, a troop ship, and trucks, reaching a staging area where he was assigned to a task force being sent into an area of North Korea known as the Chosin Reservoir, a manmade lake in the northeastern part of the country. A large Marine force had run into a massive Chinese force and was being surrounded. The Army's Seventh and Third Infantry Divisions were sent to join the fight. A regimental combat team going north would need recon support. The weather was bitterly cold and, as in the Argonne Forest six years earlier, Americans were freezing to death.

Paul rode north in the back of the truck and wondered if he had ever been colder. The temperature dropped to thirty-five below zero Fahrenheit as the task force moved into position. The air was so dry that snow mixed with dust to form an ice fog that made visibility difficult. The ground was frozen. Roads were treacherous. Marines and soldiers were dying in bloody hand to hand combat.

The Chinese leadership had ordered its forces to destroy the United Nations forces, made up mostly of Americans. The Marines had twenty-five thousand men on the line. The U.S. and British armies added another five thousand. Thirty-thousand men were facing three or four times that many Chinese forces that had been ordered to annihilate the other side.

The Chinese force surrounded the Marines, expecting capitulation. What they got was an attack that killed or wounded thousands of Chinese, who then turned their attention to the U.S. Army units, which were forced to withdraw. As the Chinese were looting the Army supplies they had captured, the Army attacked, inflicting more heavy losses on the Chinese. All of this while the American and British units were fighting their way out of the trap the Chinese thought they had sprung to end the war in their favor.

Paul was teamed with a staff sergeant named Wes Wilson, a former football player from central Pennsylvania. Wilson was a hard man. He was the kind of man who would rise to the top of an inmate population in a maximum security prison. He was sociopathic and without feelings for other human beings. He was the perfect man for the job at hand. Wilson believed that he and Paul had only the mission: to kill as many Chinese as possible in the shortest period of time. It didn't matter to him whether they were shooting at him or surrendering.

Paul and Wilson were often out beyond what passed for the lines, checking enemy positions and looking for movement on the other side. The Chinese were massing in every direction. There was no clear escape route for the Americans and the Brits and the situation was desperate. The orders had come down to withdraw to the south and bring dead and wounded with them. Chinese were overrunning American convoys and slaughtering the men in the trucks. Frozen bodies littered what passed for roads. Units were scattered all over the northeastern part of North Korea.

Paul lived in the same clothes for weeks. He wore three sets of woolen long-johns, two pairs of woolen OD (olive drab) pants, two OD shirts, three pairs of socks, leather and rubber boots, two field jackets, as many gloves as he could fit on his hand, a woolen hat and a standard-issue winter hat with earmuffs. He kept his right index finger free enough to pull the trigger on his M1. It was so cold the gun oil froze.

He wrote to Marie asking that she send him some whiskey, which was strictly forbidden. She purchased three bottles of Old Spice aftershave lotion, emptied them, filled them with liquor, and sent them as a Christmas present. Even during the dire days of December of 1950, the mail was coming in the equipment supplies that were arriving at a makeshift airfield the engineers had built.

In mid December, Paul and Wilson were watching Chinese recon teams moving toward them. Wilson opened fire, hitting one of the Chinese, and Paul fired at the others, downing one and sending another running. Wilson laughed.

"Fuckin' chinks," he said. "Let's stick around and see if they come back."

"They'll come back with mortars. Let's get out of here. I have a surprise."

The two men slipped behind a hill and found shelter from the wind in a group of large rocks. Paul reached into the pocket of his overcoat and pulled out the Old Spice bottle. "Got something."

"You gonna shave?"

Paul answered by removing the top of the bottle and taking a swig. "Here."

Wilson pulled back. "You've been on the line too long. That stuff will kill ya."

Paul snickered. "It's a little late to be thinking about dying, ain't it. Try it."

Wilson took the bottle and sniffed it. A smile came over his hard face and he put the bottle to his lips. "Damn! Best shaving lotion I ever drank."

Minutes later, the whiskey was gone and the two men were half drunk. They looked at each other and had the same thought, spoken out loud by Paul. "Let's go get us some chinks."

The battle was all around them. They had no trouble finding Chinese to shoot. They moved to the sounds of guns and screaming men. The dim light in the ice fog produced a surreal landscape of shouting and dying men. They died from bullets. They died from bayonet wounds. They died from what Army combat instructors called "horizontal butt strokes," rifle butts to the side of the head.

Paul's M1 was lost in the hand-to-hand fighting that ended with a young Chinese soldier dead of a choke that Paul had learned at the Kodokan. Paul was barely in control of himself, breathing hard and on the point of hysteria. He staggered through the fog with a bayonet in his hand, ready for another death struggle, looking for a rifle. He tripped over something and fell into the dusty snow, landing on his face. He turned and looked up and into the face of a dead Marine lying frozen and staring into the fog. The Marine was holding his M1 with both hands, his left arm frozen around the barrel, his right hand on the trigger guard. Paul needed the weapon. It took him several minutes to pry it from the frozen fingers of the Marine. As he worked, Paul looked at the man's face, which was flecked with ice. Tears rolled down his cheeks as he pulled the weapon away and checked to see that it was loaded. He took two ammo clips from the Marine, saluted, and headed back into the fight.

It would be accurate to say that Paul and Wilson were insane in those moments, driven there by conditions that normal human beings could not imagine. That day ended but the next day was no better, nor was the day after that.

Historians would describe the Battle of the Chosin Reservoir as one of the most vicious of the Twentieth Century. It was hard. It was cold. It was bloody. It was a nightmare.

Army and Marine combat engineers managed to erect bridges on the road to the port of Hungnam, where ships were being sent to evacuate the Americans. The bridges were built during the fighting and many engineers were lost.

The Americans and Brits managed to break through to Hungnam in mid-December and the evacuation began. Everything that could be loaded aboard the ships was to be taken south to deprive the Chinese of its use. The American Marines and soldiers fought every inch of the way to the port.

The last day of the evacuation was December 24th. One of the last ships to pull away was the USS General G.M. Randall, a World War Two troopship that had participated in the famous landing at Inchon earlier in the Korean War. It waited at the dock for the last of the Americans who survived the Chosin breakout.

Paul and Wilson had been assigned to guard the rear as the Americans made it to the Randall. They were to slow the Chinese to give the Americans time to pull away. It was considered a suicide assignment and both men accepted it. As it had been explained to them, "Some will die so that others may live."

The retreating troops had left mortars and machineguns at intervals to provide the troops guarding the rear with weapons and ammunition. Paul and Wilson fired the machineguns and lobbed mortar rounds in a frenzy of running and delaying and killing.

Heroes are found in unexpected places and that day the hero was the captain of the Randall, a Navy Captain who, as veterans of Chosin will tell you, had "balls of steel." He was briefed on the breakout and the evacuation and he knew that two men were the last in line and had been warned that they were expendable.

"Where are they," he asked.

"About half a kilometer out," was the reply.

"We'll wait," he said.

Paul and Wilson saw the Randall at the pier. At the rails were hundreds of Marines and soldiers, shouting and waving. They dropped everything but their M1s and ran. Sailors were at the gangplank, ready to pull it in, the ship was untied and smoke was rising from both stacks. Wilson was in front, Paul right behind. A Chinese mortar landed nearby and shrapnel blew into Paul's back and into his right lung. He kept running, blood foaming out of his mouth, and staggered aboard the ship as it pulled away. Navy gunners fired at the small Chinese unit that was making its way to the docks. Engineers had set charges to destroy what was left on the pier and explosions and smoke rose as the Randall set to sea.

The following day, Christmas Day, Paul wrote to Marie:

My Darling,

I am writing this from the General G.M. Randall. Santa Claus came yesterday and brought us a nice present. Boats. Lots of Boats. We evacuated Hungnam beachhead yesterday and came down to Pusan. Boy was I glad to get out of Hungnam. We were surrounded by more chinks than I thought existed. For a while I thought we wouldn't make it. I guess you will know about the evacuation from the papers. Well Baby, that's all the news about me.

All my love to you both,

Paul

Paul went to an Army hospital for treatment. He recovered well enough to be assigned to an administrative unit, but not the front lines. His combat days were over. He spent his time writing letters to Marie, asking her to send bathing suit photos of herself, which she did.

Wes Wilson requested and was granted another recon assignment. Paul received word that Wilson had been killed in a firefight and was being put up for a Silver Star. In his later years Paul would say that it was a proper ending for the meanest man he ever knew. He would never again speak of the Chosin fighting. When anyone brought it up, his face would tighten and he would turn away.

In December of 1951 Marie received a letter whose envelope contained a drawing of a soldier in a rowboat next to a sign at sea that read, "Frisco 7,000 miles," and the legend, "Yep, I'm coming home." Two weeks later Paul walked through the door.

Chapter twenty-five

Paul had come to the attention of Army Intelligence. His high test scores and combat experience put him a select group being considered for duty in Germany, which had become a hotbed of spies as the Cold War expanded. His amazing ability to remember details of written material put him into an even more exclusive group of men who were being assembled for duty in a special unit that would be based in Berlin.

In January of 1952 Paul reported to the Intelligence School at Ft. Holabird, Maryland, in the city of Baltimore. He learned how to pick locks, shadow people, discover if he was being shadowed, escape and evade pursuers, how to shoot someone who was holding a gun on him, how to use special cameras, and other field craft.

As he explained, "It's illegal to teach someone how to be a burglar. It is not illegal to teach someone what burglars do."

Following his training at Ft. Holabird, he was sent to Ft. Hood, Texas to learn Soviet tank doctrine. Ft. Hood is the home base of the First Armored Division. In the early fifties the Army practiced tank warfare there, pitting American armored tactics against those to be employed by the Soviets. It was the place to go to learn about Soviet tank formations, movement, and doctrine. He would be there several months, so he took Marie and Buddy with him.

The 1948 Hudson Hornet that was new to the family was large and comfortable. The trip took a week down through the South, past cotton farms where black people worked the fields, past shacks where they lived, past the "white only" signs, past the "Nigger don't let the sun set on you here" signs.

"What's wrong with people down here?" Marie asked. "Oh, my God! Look at that little girl." Marie pointed to a small child dragging a large sack through a cotton field.

Buddy was nine and just stared out the window, bored.

Paul clenched his jaw and stared ahead. This was the part of the South that he had ignored or simply blocked out.

"We should stop and visit your mother," Marie said.

"I don't think so," Paul said. "We don't have time for that."

"She's your mother."

"I'm not stopping."

"You don't even call her or write."

"I don't have anything to say to her. You know why."

The travel days began early with breakfast in a roadside diner, a stop for lunch, and dinner after dark at or near the motel where they would spend the night. Paul carried a supply of whiskey through the "dry" areas of the South, places where prohibition had never been repealed. He would lie on the bed with a glass of amber liquid and read while Marie prepared for bed and Buddy occupied himself with a toy or a game.

Each motel room had a small table and chairs. After Marie went to bed, Paul would sit with Buddy and sip his whiskey as he lectured the boy on things that most nine-year-olds don't know anything about.

"Do you know how to hold a knife in a fight?" he asked.

Buddy stared at his father.

"You don't hold it like this," Paul said, holding his arm high in the stabbing posture seen in horror movies. "It's too easy to block it. And you see here? I'm open. You hold the knife like this." He held it with the handle across his palm, blade pointing out. "You want the blade to be in a straight line from your elbow. Always forward, never sideways. A man will always telegraph his move. He'll blink his eyes or suck in his breath. When he moves, go in for the soft spots, just under the ribs or, if you can, under his chin and up through his mouth into his brain. You have that?"

Buddy tried to imagine himself in a knife fight but the thought of it scared him.

"Now, do you know how to steal food from a farmhouse if you're on the run?"

Buddy was again in new territory.

"You wait to see how many people are there. You have to wait until dawn and count them. If there's an outhouse it's easier because everyone goes to the bathroom in the morning. Then you wait for them to leave. You run into the kitchen, grab everything that's out and grabable, and get out. Never stick around or look around. Grab and go. Keep running until you're away and sure no one is following you. Then you eat the most perishable food first and save the rest. It doesn't matter what it tastes like. You're not eating at the Ritz. Got that?"

And so it went through one survival technique after another, night after night, until the Brite family arrived in Texas. Buddy retained almost none of it. He was not concerned about surviving on the run behind the Iron Curtain nor did he worry that he would be in a life-or-death knife fight any time soon.

They were in Texas for eight months. Paul finished his armor training and was sent to another intelligence school at Ft. Sill, Oklahoma, where he learned specialized map making, using unique inks, papers, and other substances designed to fool Soviet interior and border guards who were tasked with finding and eliminating American spies.

Just before Christmas the family headed north to deposit Marie and Buddy in Massachusetts before Paul went off to Berlin to begin his new assignment. Night after night, Paul sat Buddy down to listen to a drunken lecture about survival.

"Let's say a guy from the other side has you with your hands up and is moving in on you. What do you do?"

"I don't know," Buddy said.

"First, always, and I mean always, keep a loose cigarette in your shirt pocket. Relax. Act like you have no idea why the guy is pointing the thing at you. Look confused. What do confused people do? They calmly, I mean calmly, reach into their shirt pocket for a cigarette. It's a natural thing to do. You might even say, 'Hey, I'm just getting a smoke.' Then what do guys who've got an unlit cigarette in their mouths do? They reach for their lighter in their front pants pocket. That's where I keep the Derringer or a Baretta or some other small handgun. They don't pack much punch and they're not very accurate, but if you're close, they'll do the job. The guy thinks I'm getting the lighter and I've got him."

"Where's the gun?" Buddy asked.

"I don't have one of those yet but I will when I need it."

"Can I see it when you get it?"

"You bet."

"Okay."

"Listen, Buddy, I'm going away for a while but you and Mother will be joining me in Germany. But between now and then I need you to be the man around here. She's a pretty woman and she'll be getting' attention from some of those slobs in Lowell. You need to watch out and make sure everything's okay. Got that?"

Buddy nodded his head. "Watch out for what?"

"Just watch out."

Chapter twenty-six

Paul arrived in Berlin in January of 1953. The city had more spies per square mile than any other city on Earth. The former capital of the Third Reich had been carved into four sectors by the victors of the war against Germany. The United States, Britain and France represented the interests of those who had been on the Western Front. The Soviet Union has taken the city in 1945 and had the largest sector, almost as large as the other three combined.

The Western powers had implemented a plan to rebuild the city and new office and apartment towers were going up on the blocks where nothing but rubble had been left when the war ended. The Soviets had lost millions of citizens to the Nazis and were in no mood to be nice to the Germans and left the rubble as a lesson in what happens when Russia's enemies move against the Motherland. The Western powers installed democratic government structures and urged the Germans to move past the Nazi era. The Soviets were unforgiving and harsh and imposed a strict and brutal system in what became known as East Berlin. Neither side trusted the other and both sides expected trouble, even war, as tensions grew.

It was a situation ripe for intrigue and a fertile ground for cloak and dagger work. Intelligence Collection Group/Berlin Station was housed in an estate on the outskirts of the American sector. The estate's primary building, a mansion that represented the tastes of the old German ruling class, had survived the allied bombings and was ideal for its new purpose. The old tapestries, suits of armor, swords and paintings had been removed during the war and were stored in warehouses that the Americans had liberated and were only now being assessed.

The primary rooms of the mansion were furnished with government-issue desks and chairs and the walls were covered with maps and photographs showing the known position of Soviet units in what had come to be known as East Germany, or, as the Soviets preferred, the Deutsche Demokratische Republik, known to Americans as the German Democratic Republic or DDR.

It was not an ideal headquarters location for many reasons, not the least of which was the ease with which it could be bugged. It was not a "secure" building by any reasonable standard, given its open position, many windows, and history as a part-time residence for high-level Nazis who—it was assumed—had been bugged by the Gestapo. The Army full colonel who ran Intelligence Collection Group/Berlin was no fool. His name was Harvel P. Flummery and he had spent his entire life fending off jokes about his name. He wore a brushy mustache, a scowl, smoked a pipe, and had an unusual ability to assemble the right men for any given job.

He gazed out the window of his office as the new men were brought in. Three of them were former uniform soldiers who had seen combat and therefore could be counted upon to stand and fight should the situation arise. He turned and looked at the four men standing at his desk. They were all at attention even though everyone was wearing civilian clothes.

"At ease, men. We don't adhere to military protocol in this unit, so forget salutes and standing at attention and all that. You're not in the infantry anymore."

"Yes, sir," the all responded.

"And that, too. You'll call me Harv. That does not mean we're friends."

"Yes, sir."

Flummery let it pass. "You've all been trained so you know the basics but you don't know the game. You'll learn it soon enough. We're watching the other side and they're watching us. They're probably recording this meeting. If so, comrades, *ya bystro gavaryu?* Am I speaking too fast? He hollered to the ceiling. He walked to a table-model radio and tuned it to a classical music program and turned up the volume. "It drives them crazy," he said.

He motioned for all four men to come closer. "Upstairs are rooms with desks. Each of you will have one to use as your own. Each desk will have a name and a file. I want you all to go up, find your desk, and read the file. Later, we'll go for individual walks and discuss your assignments. That is all."

All four men had been chosen because they each possessed a special talent that was needed for the work at hand. Paul had an extraordinary memory, was a speed reader, and an experienced fighter.

A man named Tex Dougherty was a skilled mechanic who could quickly disable or repair any type of vehicle, including those currently in use by the Soviets. Tex was, naturally, from Texas and had grown up on a ranch near Corpus Christi. He was tough, used to hard work, and had been in more than a few fistfights, not to mention his service as one of General Patton's tank repairmen.

Junior Gaston was from Chicago and had been too young to fight in the Second World War. He had been drafted at the age of twenty and had come to the attention of Army Intelligence because he had an unnatural ability to remember numbers. Gaston could scan a page of numbers that represented an encrypted document and recall, twenty four hours later, every number on the page in the correct order and spacing. He was a savant, a person with one extraordinary skill. He was lacking in other areas, however, and could not learn to drive a car. Army Intelligence was happy to assign him a driver.

Steve Wargo was a Hungarian-American whose parents were acclaimed musicians. They had found a home in New York when Steve was a small boy. He grew up in a world of culture, education, and the Hungarian language. Hungary was one of the Eastern European nations that had fallen under the Soviet yoke and American Intelligence was gathering information, recruiting agents and, when possible, stirring up trouble for the Soviets. Wargo was an ideal agent for what was happening in Budapest.

The files the men were given were assessments of the current situation in the region around Berlin. The city was an island, a special zone, in the Soviet-controlled area of Germany. All access to and from the city was controlled by the Soviets who were fond of harassing Westerners whom they viewed as spies, military or civilian. They controlled the rail lines to the West and routinely searched trains carrying U.S. military personnel, prompting a round of protests which produced the occasional apology or even a claim of some "misunderstanding," but the harassment continued and was accepted as part of life in that part of the world.

What concerned Colonel Flummery was what was happening to the east, in the German countryside where the Soviets and their Eastern European allies had military installations. The American government was concerned that the Soviets would launch an attack on Western Europe to gain control of the continent's resources and, in the bargain, assert the alleged superiority of the Communist system.

Flummery's task was to keep an eye on the Russians and assess their military intentions. To do that he had his own agents and those he could recruit among the Germans who were chafing at the controls the Russians had in place. His four new men would join his team to do just that.

Berlin was a city of checkpoints. Leaving or entering a sector required a stop, the presentation of relevant papers, a clearance, then another inspection a few yards away, even going from the American zone to the British or French. Everyone assumed that everyone else was a spy for one party or another. Movement into or out of the Soviet zone was harsh at times and it was not unusual for the person crossing the zone line to be detained. Woe be unto the one who was taken for interrogation to one of the many police or military facilities the Soviets had set up in their area.

Actual spies, the ones who were the reasons for the checkpoints, avoided all of this through means of tunnels beneath the streets of Berlin. The Nazis had built a series of bomb shelters. Many of the apartment and office buildings in the city had connecting basements that were built long before Hitler came to power. There was a maze beneath the city that intelligence agencies used to ferry agents from one place to another.

The Western powers used them and so did the Soviets. Each side tried to find the other's underground transit points and block them. In some cases, both sides used the same tunnels and that produced the occasional awkward moment.

American military intelligence had dug its own tunnel that was not shared with anyone, even American allies. The tunnel was dug by Army engineers using the cover of the noise of above ground construction to hide the noise of the underground digging. It was actually two tunnels running from one spot in the American sector to two locations in the Soviet sector. The tunnels began and ended in the basements of ordinary apartment buildings that had no distinguishing features. The buildings offered easy access to busy intersections and transit points. It was an ideal way of getting agents into or out of Soviet-controlled territory.

Colonel Flummery wasted no time with the new men. "Go to this address. Show them the identification papers you're carrying and do what you're told."

Paul and the other men were wearing civilian clothing they had been told to purchase in the U.S. It was standard suit-and-tie stuff that fit poorly and looked cheap. Each man had been given one-hundred dollars cash and told to purchase an entire wardrobe, so each man was a testament to bargain quality. It might have satisfied the military types at Ft. Holabird but it wouldn't fool anyone in a European city who knew quality. In Flummery's estimation, the men had GI-in-civvies written all over them.

The address was a tailor who was skilled at making custom men's clothing that could present the wearer as, say, an East German or a Russian. He could add or subtract qualities that made suits baggy, ill-fitting, well-tailored, or whatever the need at hand. Flummery wanted his men to look good and put together in a mid-quality sense. He didn't want to them to stand out as aristocrats but he didn't want them to look shabby and ill-mannered, either.

The tailor was good and he was fast. Within three days all four men had wardrobes that blended in with what passed for well-dressed in post-war Berlin: well-fitting sport coats of good quality wool, tailored slacks, crisp white shirts, silk ties, and gold cufflinks. Flummery told the men to let their hair grow out of the military cuts they were wearing and into something a bit more stylish.

When the four appeared in his office in their new clothing, he pointed to the ceiling and said, "The problem with Russians is they all look like they're wearing their father's clothes. Nothing fits. And they have borscht stains all over their shirts." He waved for the men to follow him. "Let's visit the armory."

Paul and the other men followed Flummery downstairs into a basement room that reeked of age and water leaks. Gun racks, foot lockers, wooden shipping crates and assorted leather bags were hanging on the walls or placed upon makeshift tables.

"We need to get this out of here before every weapon in the place gets rusty, but it's here for now. Each of you will get your own basic load, as we used to say in the infantry. For you, Tex, it's mouse-gun, a primary handgun, brass knuckles and a blackjack. Junior, you get the handguns and lock picking tools. Brite, you and Wargo will get the full load plus a few other things. Now take off your jackets." "Mouse-gun" was a term used for a very small handgun.

The men removed their new custom sport coats and held them over their arms. Flummery took Paul's coat and held it up. "This looks like any other sport coat you'd see on the street. Our man has made a few modifications to meet our, meaning your, needs." He picked up a Walther P38. "This, as you know, is the standard German military handgun. It replaced the Luger. It's a nine millimeter weapon and carries an eight round magazine. The round leaves the muzzle at twelve-hundred feet per second. It will, I stress will, bring a man down. If, that is, you hit him. It is your basic weapon."

Flummery tossed the weapon to Paul and motioned for him to come closer. "We don't want you men to wear shoulder holsters because they're bulky, easily seen, and call attention to you. So where do you carry the Walther? Brite, find the vertical opening to the left of the inside pocket of the jacket."

Paul took a moment to find it and he held it open for the others to see. Flummery slid the Walther into the opening and told Paul to put the jacket on. "See, there's no bulge. Our man has created a built-in, cloth holster. The weapon is supported by the entire upper part of the jacket, not just a pocket, so it doesn't cause a bulge. It will be discovered if you're frisked, of course, but if that happens you're already in trouble." He handed each man a Walther. "Put them in your coats."

The afternoon wore on with each man being issued what the Army Intelligence leadership in Berlin felt he needed. Paul was issued a .25 caliber Colt 1908 Hammerless handgun as a "mouse-gun" or "pocket gun." It was just over four inches long and weighed thirteen ounces. He was to keep it in his right front pocket. He was also issued a set of top quality lock-picking tools, small, black brass knuckles, and a blackjack. The blackjack was seven inches long with a leather-covered, egg-sized lead ball at one end and a marble-size lead ball at the other. The lead balls were connected by a tightly wound steel spring.

"Brite and Wargo, you have the option of a British commando knife if you like. You'll have to carry it on your leg. I have the scabbard and straps." Paul took the knife. It was one of the most lethal knives ever made. Overall, the knife is just over eleven inches in length, but the blade takes up seven inches. It tapers to a point that its designers intended as a tool to penetrate a man's ribcage and sever his primary arteries. It was manufactured by the famous Wilkinson Sword Company and was used with great effect by British commandos in the war.

Their custom clothing hid most of the weapons and other issued items. The Walther made the coats heavier by almost two pounds but there was no alternative other than to abandon the weapon, which was unthinkable.

Armed with two handguns, a fighting knife, a blackjack, brass knuckles, and lock picking tools, Paul was ready for his first assignment.

"Gentlemen, welcome to Berlin." Flummery had a smile on his face.

Chapter twenty-seven

Paul and Steve Wargo were told to walk around
Berlin to learn the city and get accustomed to the weight
and feel of their clothing and equipment. Paul walked
with a rolling, country boy gate that did not match the
hurried city pace that Berliners and others accustomed to
sidewalks employed. It seemed to Wargo that Paul took
one step while everyone else took two, although Paul
kept pace.

"The way you walk will make it easy to follow
you," Wargo said. "You roll your shoulders from side to
side."

Paul tried to alter his gate and take smaller steps. It
made him look like someone who was practicing
walking, and this made him stand out even more.

Berlin was coming back to life eight years after the
end of the war and cafes were popular with the
international crowd, Berliners, military personnel from a
dozen nations, and spies who were observing friends and
foes. The coffee was good, the pastries were better, and
everyone smoked.

Paul and Wargo looked around at the others in the
cafe and tried to pick out the spies. Half the place was
suspect. They assumed they were easy to spot because
they still had their military haircuts. They also assumed
that the spies in the café were taking their pictures and
creating files. It was the way things were done when
new faces were spotted.

Berlin in January is cold and dark. The city enjoys less than eight hours of daylight and endures sixteen hours of darkness in the winter, the reverse in the summer. But in January of 1953 the darkness was welcome for the spies who infested the city. Darkness offers cover. A man can hide.

Paul and Wargo rode with Flummery in a government-owned Mercedes to a streetcar stop where a driver dropped them off. The three men then boarded *die Straßenbahn* and rode for fifteen minutes to a stop on a block of apartment buildings that had been refurbished after the war. They walked in a zigzag pattern, checking to see if they were being followed. After two blocks they turned into an alley where three bicycles had been left for them. They pedaled the bicycles another eight blocks, turning a series of rights and lefts to shake off anyone following them.

One of the basic ways of shaking a tale is by bicycle. Intelligence trainers tell their students that a bike is too fast for someone trailing them on foot and too slow for someone trailing by car. A bike was a common form of transportation in Berlin at the time and no one paid much attention to the three men.

Another alley offered shelter for the bikes and the men left them against a wall and walked to the front door of an apartment building and rang a buzzer for an apartment on the fourth floor. The men entered, climbed the stairs, and found an open door to the apartment. Whoever was in the apartment had gone to a room and closed the door and was not visible to the three men who walked to a back bedroom, opened a closet door, and stepped inside. In the rear of the closet a hidden doorway led to a narrow stairwell that had been built between the apartment walls and the outer wall of the building. It was barely wide enough for a man to pass.

The three moved quietly down the hidden stairs to a small basement room that was lined with wooden packing boxes stuffed with excelsior, wood shavings that were common packing material. The idea was that a casual observer would think the room was used for storage. Behind the boxes was a metal door that was locked in four places.

Flummery signaled Paul. "Let's see what you can do with those locks."

Paul took his wallet from his back pocket and removed his lock picking tools. He inserted them into the first lock and heard it open. At Ft. Holabird, the students had been required to get through a dozen locks in less than a minute and he had no trouble opening the door.

The tunnel was dark. Army engineers had reinforced the tunnel walls and ceiling with the metal grating that was designed for makeshift runways on muddy fields. The grating was strong, if rough to the eye. Flummery used a flashlight to guide them about a hundred yards to another wall and another locked door. This time he signaled for Wargo to pick the locks.

The process was the reverse of their descent into the underground. This time they climbed a different set of secret stairs to an apartment where a door to a closet was waiting. Within minutes they were on the sidewalk in the Soviet sector, which was dark and empty of foot or vehicle traffic. The Soviets did not encourage citizens under its control to go out, not that there was much to do in their sector.

"There's a curfew over here. Most people are not allowed on the streets when it's dark. That's kind of a challenge this time of year when it's dark most of the time," Flummery whispered, taking Paul and Wargo by their arms and guiding them to a pre-war Mercedes that bore Soviet military license plates. "Get in."

A young man dressed in a Red Army uniform was behind the wheel. He put the car in gear and pulled away from the curb.

"*Davayte korotkiy tur*," Flummery said in Russian. Let's take the short tour.

"Yes, sir," the driver said in perfect English.

"*Govorit' tol'ko v Rossii*," Speak only in Russian. Flummery opened the glove compartment and handed papers to Paul and Wargo. "These will get you through the checkpoints. You're Swiss observers. Don't say anything."

Paul looked at his papers and saw his photo and identification in French and German. Wargo glanced at his papers and slid them into the inside pocket of his sport coat.

Snow began to fall as the car cruised to the outskirts of the Soviet sector and into a Red Army roadblock. Their papers were examined by bored-looking soldiers who waved them on. The tour took two hours during which Paul and Wargo observed the workings of the new German police state being assembled by their masters in Moscow. Some of the side roads were blocked with warning signs and armed guards.

"Down those roads are the Soviet military units you'll be keeping an eye on. They're not as husky as they look. The Russians like their vodka in cold weather and the guards are pretty gooney by midnight. You'd have to fall over them to be noticed. You'll figure it out." Flummery said something in a low voice to the driver and soon they were back at the apartment building where they had come up from the American Sector. "Think of this as an introduction," he said. "It won't be long before you'll know the Russian sector as well as you know your own home town."

Flummery's drills lasted another two weeks. Paul and Steve were sent to the Soviet sector at different times of the day. They went together and by themselves. Each time they were met by a driver wearing Soviet military clothing driving a pre-war car with Soviet military identification. Each time they were handed papers identifying them as international observers. They passed through Soviet roadblocks, offering their papers, and cruised the streets of East Berlin. The Russians were making no attempt to mask their hatred of the Germans. Some of the streets were barely passable eight years after the war. Buildings were left in ruins. The skeletons of dead animals were left in place. Signs in front of bombed buildings read, *Ruhm zu den kommunistischen Leuten.* Glory to communist people.

And *Marxismus/Leninismus ordnen die Welt an.* Marxism/Leninism will rule the world.

Paul and Wargo didn't care about the signs. They were paying attention to the Soviets and their East German minions, some of whom were taking on the characteristics of their masters. The Stasi, known formally as the Ministry for State Security, the East German secret police, were creating as much terror as the NKVD, the precursor to the KGB. Midnight knocks on the door were common and summary executions of those deemed "anti-revolutionary" were common. Some of those being shot were agents recruited by Flummery's men.

Paul and Wargo spent hours at a firing range that was set up for the agents to become familiar with the weapons they carried. For Paul, it was a highlight of his work. He liked guns, knew them well, and fired thousands of rounds at silhouette and bulls eye targets, fruit, bottles, cans, and windows. He refreshed his hand-to-hand skills and engaged in rough sparring with self-defense experts. He was taught how and where to use the blackjack. He was taught how to fight with brass knuckles which, he was told, were to protect his hands, not kill his opponent. If he wanted to use lethal force, he should use a firearm or his commando knife.

A month into his time in Berlin, he was summoned to Flummery's office. As usual, Flummery greeted him by shouting at the ceiling for the benefit of the Soviets who were bugging the room. "We're just having a little conversation, comrades. You can take a moment to buy yourselves suits that fit." He then turned up the radio to allow Wagner to drown out what he had to say to Paul.

"I have a little something for you. Little is the key word." He handed Paul a small, round object. "It's a Petal camera, the smallest in the world." The camera was just a little larger than a quarter and half an inch thick. "It has a fixed focus lens and takes six photographs on twenty-five millimeter film. Here are some cassettes for it. Insert them in the back and turn this piece to rotate to the next frame. Simple. You can keep it in your pocket with your change. Any questions?"

"What am I going to do with it?"

"You are going to take photographs of our friends on the other side. In the beginning you'll practice by taking pictures of their military units in the field. Later, you'll be using your lock-picking skills to get documents or photos of documents. Spend the day getting to know it. Indoor shots will require a flashlight. Take some pictures around here and leave them in the lab upstairs. They'll process them and we can go over them together to see how you're doing. We need to get going on this. You're training time is about over. We need you in the field."

Paul held the small, silver-colored camera. There was a small view finder and a push-down lever on one side. The lever snapped the photograph. "I'll get right to it."

He spent the day snapping photos of the grounds around the mansion and taking interior shots of the furniture. He brought the cassettes to the lab and had prints that night. The exterior shots were acceptably clear but the interior photos were either out of focus or they were too dark. He practiced with the camera for three days and learned how to capture images that an analyst could read.

On a gloomy Saturday morning, with the dawn breaking at eight o'clock, Paul slipped into East Berlin. The forecast was for a cloudy day with light snow and temperatures in the twenties. He had been learning basic German and could read street signs and ask for directions. He could order coffee. He had memorized the address of a safe house where he could go if he got into trouble. He had memorized the name on his papers and a few basic facts about the person he purported to be.

His driver took him to a Soviet headquarters area and pulled to the side of the road. The driver got out and acted anxious. He raised the hood of the Mercedes he was driving and tinkered with the engine, poking here and there.

Paul got out and looked around like someone whose car had broken down. He reached into his shirt pocket and took out a cigarette. He reached into his pants pocket and pulled out his lighter, making a show of turning away from the wind to light up. The Petal camera was in the palm of his hand as he held the light and he snapped a photo as he flipped open the top of the Zippo, a prize even among the communists. He advanced the film as he closed the lighter, turned, and snapped another photo.

The driver said something and closed the hood and Mercedes moved away from the Soviet area. So it went for several hours. The next day Flummery and Paul went over the photos and analyzed them for intelligence. It was Paul's routine until the first signs of spring. When the snow melted and the danger of tracks disappeared with it, Paul was told to prepare to break into Soviet military buildings. The big leagues were calling.

Chapter twenty-eight

Colonel Flummery called a meeting of the new men in a secure conference room at the U.S. Army Headquarters/Berlin. The room was furnished with government-issue metal chairs lined up in four rows, a raised desk in front, and a pull-down screen over a blackboard. He stood behind the desk as the four men walked in.

"Up here, men. Take seats in the front." He motioned for them to step up. "Sit."

"I've called you here to give you the big picture, so to speak. I want you to know how you fit in to the overall mission here in Berlin and, indeed, in West Germany." He pulled down a map showing all of the powers that controlled Europe, East and West.

Paul whispered to Wargo, "Gotta love the big picture pony show."

"Wake me up when it gets interesting," Wargo said

"The North Atlantic Treaty Organization, NATO, is comprised of the Western victors from World War Two plus Germany. The big dog in NATO is the United States, with Britain, France and the others taking lesser roles, but they don't like it when we point that out. NATO's reason for being is to protect Western Europe from the Warsaw Pact—whose big dog is the Soviet Union—the lesser nation's being East Germany, Poland and other so-called 'captive' nations." He pointed to the

Eastern European nations over which the Soviet hammer and sickle had been superimposed.

"NATO's assumption is that should the Warsaw Pact make its move, it will come in the form of a massive tank attack through the Fulda Gap, strategic low ground that runs from East Germany all the way to Frankfurt am Mein in the heart of West Germany." Flummery pulled down another map with arrows marking the Fulda Gap. "This gap contains two corridors suitable for massive tank attacks. The northern route through the Gap passes south of the Knüllgebirge and then continues past the Vogelsberg Mountains, as you see here. The southern route passes through the Fliede and Kinzig Valleys." He slapped the map to indicate the routes he had outlined. "We and they know that the most tank-friendly route is the North German Plain, not the Gap, but it's a longer route and the Soviets believe their only chance of success is a quick strike that succeeds before we can react. So that's what we're keeping an eye on."

Wargo made a snoring sound.

Flummery stopped talking and looked at Paul, Wargo, Tex Dougherty and Junior Gaston. He wanted to gauge their attention and their understanding. "I don't have to remind you that this briefing is top secret. Some of what I'm telling you is known to both sides and has even been in the paper. Some of it has not."

All four men nodded and stared at the maps.

"NATO planners assume that the Fulda Gap is a natural avenue for the massive Soviet tank divisions that vastly outnumbered their NATO counterparts. There are many in NATO who believe that should such an attack be launched there is little NATO can do short of a nuclear response, given the numerical superiority of the Warsaw Pact."

He raised the maps and brought up a slide showing Soviet armored units massed in a field near Berlin. Paul recognized it as a photo he had taken.

"Conventional wisdom has it that NATO's tanks are better. But quality costs more. Soviet tanks are junk but there are many thousands of them and even if each NATO tank knocked out five Soviet tanks, there are plenty more Soviet tanks to take their place and achieve an ultimate victory, so the thinking goes here at headquarters." He looked at the men. "Any questions so far?"

Paul raised his hand. "How do we fit in?"

"I'm getting to that," Flummery said. He tapped the photo of the tanks.

"Your mission is to keep an eye on the Soviets and, if an attack appears imminent, our plan is to strike first and hard. That's where you fellows come into the picture. It's your job to know if and when the Soviets will make their move. It requires constant surveillance, analysis, and, often, guesswork. It's time to get to work."

Flummery again looked at the men sitting before him and wished he had a pitcher of cold water to throw on them.

"With the snow gone, it's easier to approach the Soviet areas without leaving tracks that would be easy to follow. The Soviet tanks units are massed outside Berlin in a line back to the Polish border. Thousands of tanks are lined up in fields where eight years ago the Red Army crashed into Germany in a white hot fury of vengeance and retribution. Russian anger over the millions lost in the Great Patriotic War has not subsided. German citizens are second class on their own soil. That's good news for us."

He clapped his hands. "You men still with me?"

All four nodded and murmured.

Paul whispered, "It will all be over before this damn briefing ends."

"Sergeant Brite, is there something you would like to add?"

"No, Sir."

"Let's move on. As I was saying about Soviet attitudes toward their German allies, it's a weakness. The Russian's just don't like the Germans, even the ones who make up the new East German Army. The Russians don't trust the Poles, Hungarians, Latvians or any of the other member nations. Control remains with Moscow in all areas. Soviet tanks are not massed with the tanks of other nations. Local Soviet commanders have no authority to do anything more important take orders. The Red Army massed right now as a threat against the West is a powerful giant whose brain is someplace else."

Paul wondered if his Soviet counterparts were being subjected to this kind of briefing and hearing a senior officer talk about the Americans and their allies and how the West German's felt about the United States. *Probably*, he concluded. He also assumed that no German, East or West, was fond of their conqueror, no matter where they came from. But that wasn't his concern.

Paul had been in the field under extreme conditions and had no fear about his mission. He knew how to maneuver against an enemy and he could take care of himself. His only concern was whether he would gather the correct information. The Soviets knew men like Paul were operating in their territory. They had their own field spies in West Germany snooping around, taking pictures, and recruiting agents. Each side played games with the other and attempted to mask what they were doing with their forces, but it's difficult to hide what thousands of men and vehicles are up to.

Paul obtained a trench coat with a wool lining as protection against the wet, cold German winter, which was fading but still miserable. He purchased a fedora to both warm his head and protect it against the rain and snow. He caught a glimpse of himself in a storefront window and chucked. He looked like a caricature of a spy. He mugged to himself, flexing his fists and making a serious, spy-like face. There was an instant when the Southern boy he had been came to the surface, the kid who laughed and knew no war. The kid returned to the past and Paul walked down the gloomy street and into the apartment building that would take him to the other side.

This time his driver was an older man who was behind the wheel of a pre-war Opel Kapitan, a four-door sedan that offered the luxury of a heater with a blower. This one was black and bore local license plates. The driver was a serious-faced fellow with a chubby face. He did not acknowledge Paul as he climbed into the back seat. The driver pulled away from the curb and spent half an hour making right and left turns to shake anyone who might have been following. He then drove out of the city along a two-lane road that was lined with trees. He came to a cross road and stopped.

"I meet you here two hour," he said in a heavy accent.

Paul got out and the car sped away. He looked at his map and saw symbols that represented his mission. He left the road and made his way through the trees, following a path that was little used but still visible. He expected to hear someone call out and challenge him but no such challenge was issued, so he continued to walk until he came to a barbed wire fence and a series of signs. *Achtung! Aufmerksamkeit! kein Zugang! halten Sie weg!* Attention. No access. Go away. There was a painted image of a rifle pointing at the viewer. It was a clear warning that anyone crossing the fence would be shot.

Paul looked around and saw no one. He climbed over the fence and waited. No one called out. He moved down the fence and away from the path, listening for the sound of guards or dogs. He heard nothing but the normal sounds of the woods; birds, wind, rustling leaves. It was mid-afternoon. It would be dark soon. He needed to get to a spot where he could see his target before he lost the light. He moved away from the fence, staying near tall trees and thick brush that could offer shelter from observers.

After two hundred yards he heard what sounded like engines starting and as he moved closer he could hear men shouting. He slowly made his way to the sound and saw that he was near a large field where Soviet tanks and half-tracks were parked in rows. Small groups of soldiers were going from vehicle to vehicle, starting them and letting them idle for a few minutes, then shutting them down. It was the kind of thing crews everywhere did in cold weather when they weren't going anywhere.

He took the Petal camera out of his pocket and snapped two cassettes of pictures. He also drew a crude map of the formations and counted heads among the crews. He waited for thirty minutes, watching the field, and saw that the crews kept vodka in the tanks and relaxed and drank as the sun set. Flummery had been correct. The Russians liked their vodka and felt safe enough to get drunk without worrying about the Americans.

Paul's routine was set. He would go into the Soviet zone, meet a driver, and observe and photograph military bases. His photos and drawings would be incorporated into maps that monitored Soviet troop and armor movements.

Steve Wargo was spending time in Hungary on the same type mission. Paul had no idea what Junior Gaston was doing but it certainly involved numbers and some form of encryption. Tex Dougherty was often away and word had it that he was examining Soviet military vehicles and devising methods of disabling them quickly or otherwise creating problems for their crews.

In the late spring of 1953 the Soviet system being imposed on East Germans was beginning to unravel. Moscow had decreed that East Germany contribute huge amounts of its resources to the military. Add to that huge reparations payments from the war and the country was left destitute, with its Soviet masters demanding more from the workers while imposing pay cuts.

The Soviets had found a lackey named Walter Ulbricht to lead the country and he was ordered to carry out his instructions to the letter, no matter the brutality or suffering it caused. East Germans were staging strikes and the Soviets were moving men and tanks.

Flummery called another meeting, this one was attended by men Paul had never seen before. He stood on the stage holding a pointer in both hands and watched as his spies found seats. He waited until the idle chatter ended and he looked at each man.

"All hell is about to break loose," he said. "East Germans don't have enough to eat. They don't have heat and for a good period of each they don't even have electricity. We believe, although the Soviets don't, that the situation will explode. We can only guess what the Soviets will do. Stalin is dead and there's a leadership struggle at the Kremlin. This guy Ulbricht is supposed to be some kind of strongman for them in Germany but he's as clueless as any of them. Frankly, these guys have only one answer to everything and it's the hammer. When in doubt, shoot. That's their one and only plan. Our plan is make sure things get as nasty as possible for our friends on the other side. To do that we need every one of you in the field. Some of you will be keeping an eye on things, others will be making whatever mischief you can, and Tex here will run up their vehicle repair bill." There was a small chuckle in the group.

"We've got the entire team on this. The guys in uniform are on alert all over West Germany and we don't know if the Soviets will use the trouble on their side as an excuse to make a move against us." Flummery pulled down a map and spent an hour going over what was known about the position of Soviet units. When the briefing ended he pointed to Paul. "Brite, stick around. The rest of you can pick up your packets upstairs."

Paul stood and lit a cigarette as he watched the others leave the briefing room. "What's up?"

"How are you doing with the cameras?"

"You tell me."

"We need a bit of work done and you're the man to do it. The Soviets have been moving a lot of couriers between Berlin and Moscow and we think they're issuing orders about how to handle the East Germans if things get nasty. We need to get our hands on those orders. What do you think?"

"About?"

"Going in and taking a few pictures."

"Where?"

"Your old stomping grounds. They've got some brass settled in at armored headquarters twenty kilometers east of Berlin. They think they can fool us into thinking it's all happening at their headquarters in the city but we have reliable information that the tankers will take the lead on whatever happens and that's where they've got the generals who'll run this thing. Do you think you can get inside?"

"Only one way to find out." Paul was smiling.

Chapter twenty-nine

All military headquarters were alike in Paul's opinion. They called attention to themselves by their nature. Generals don't like to hide their lights under bushels, so they surround themselves with the things that announced to the world that they're important. Things like flags, special cars, well-dressed aides, guards, runners and men whose only job is to make the high ranking officers feel important. It was no different with the Soviets. Finding the headquarters was no challenge whether the Red Army was or was not trying to hide its intentions.

The armored divisions outside Berlin were humming like bees near a hive. Tanks and Soviet versions of jeeps were moving into and out of formations, soldiers were wearing full battle gear and marching to the screams of NCOs, and small aircraft were flying overhead. Paul assumed that the same things were happening at American bases in the west.

He was at the tree line of a base he had been scouting, using a pair of Zeiss binoculars that were popular with both the Americans and the Russians. German officers had carried them during the war and they were considered the best in the world. The pair Paul was using had been liberated from a Wehrmacht Colonel at war's end. They were military-grade and were useful in determining distance. Paul assumed the Soviets who were supposed to be scanning the woods for people like him were also carrying Zeiss binoculars, although no one seemed to be paying much attention to the tree line at the moment.

He watched the activity on the base and observed how the headquarters building was protected. The Soviets apparently felt there was no threat because security was light and appeared to be for show rather than perceived threats. He noticed that the soldiers guarding the entrance to the building were carrying unloaded Kalashnikovs slung over their shoulders. The guards' primary purpose appeared to be standing at attention and saluting the officers who went in and out.

Paul took that as a sign that security inside was likely to be loose. The sun set and the officers climbed into automobiles to the salutes of the guards and men in the ranks and soon the bullet-less guards were the only ones near the headquarters building. After an hour or so the guards stepped down from their positions of attention and lit cigarettes while they chatted. By midnight the guards were passing around flasks of vodka.

An officer of the guard made his rounds, inspected his men, and drove away. The guards then sat down on the steps near the door and fell asleep. Paul knew he had a short window to accomplish his task. The hours between one and four in the morning are when men are least alert, so he had to move.

He slipped between the tanks, staying in the shadows cast by the weak lights that were positioned on poles at the ends of the formations. He was on alert for stray soldiers who may have been assigned guard duty among the tanks or those who were drunk and staggering through the parked vehicles. He reasoned that if the guards had no ammunition, neither would ordinary soldiers walking around, but he didn't want to test that theory.

The only light near the headquarters building was a spotlight that had been mounted over the door to illuminate the entrance. The rest of the area was dark. Two Soviet jeeps were parked end to end near the entrance and they offered cover as he slipped closer. The guards were snoring on the steps. The building had three entrances. The primary entrance was in the front and had two doors, side by side. There was another entrance in the rear and one on the right side as Paul faced the building. The side and rear entrances were single steel doors that were in complete darkness.

He moved to the rear to get as much distance as possible between him and the sleeping guards. He didn't want to take the risk that one of them would need to relieve himself and come around to the side of the building and find an American breaking in. He had no trouble picking the lock and moving inside to a short flight of stairs that led to a hallway. He had a small flashlight and moved down the hallway looking for a door that would tell him that a high ranking officer was using the office on the other side. He found a door that was marked by a single star, the insignia of a Soviet major general. Next to it was another door with two stars, a lieutenant general. And next to that was a door with three stars, a colonel general. This was the man who was in charge.

The door was secured by three locks of a heavy-duty deadbolt design. Paul smiled. His instructors at Ft. Holabird had plenty of these locks for the students to practice on. The students were required to get through a dozen of them in a timed exercise. He was in the office in less than thirty seconds.

It took him five minutes to find the secure metal file cabinet marked *сверхсекретный* in red. He had seen it many times on documents that had been taken from the Soviets and knew it meant top secret. He picked the lock on the cabinet and retrieved all of the documents that were marked classified. He used the flashlight to illuminate them as he snapped pictures with the Petal camera. Fifteen minutes later he put the documents back into their folders and locked the file cabinet. He took photos of the office before he locked the door. An hour later he was on a one lane dirt road signaling his driver.

By nine o'clock in the morning analysts were reading the documents and by noon the highest ranking American, British and French military leaders were being briefed on Soviet plans to ruthlessly crush any attempt at rebellion by the East Germans. The documents contained no suggestion that a move against the West was under consideration.

Berlin was tense as spring came to an end. The Soviets had no sympathy for the Germans or their suffering. The economy in the East continued to collapse. German workers saw their pay reduced. Essential commodities were scarce or nonexistent. Soviet tanks were as common as automobiles on the streets of East Berlin. Flummery's men were busy, trying to assess Soviet intentions and the options for the West.

Paul was given new clothes tailored to look like the clothing being worn by East Germans of lower middle class. He wore a cheap imitation leather jacket, poor quality trousers, and shoes that had no elegance.

Flummery gave him a Soviet-made camera called a Zorki that was a near-replica of the famous Leica C3 that was considered the best 35mm camera in the world. The Zorki was lower quality but it was the best choice for camera buffs behind what was being called The Iron Curtain, a term coined by Winston Churchill.

Paul spent his days and nights posing as an East German with time on his hands, walking around and snapping photos of famous sites and the ruins left by the war. His photos had Soviet tanks or military units somewhere in the frame, although to a casual eye he appeared to be interested in something else. He memorized street patterns and gauged Soviet level of interest in various neighborhoods they controlled.

His German was better and he could carry on basic conversations but he pronounced German words with a distinct Alabama accent, making his encounters with Russians chancy. He tried to steer clear of the East German roadblocks where it would be clear that he was an American. Russians in East Germany also had limited German vocabularies and spoke with a heavy Russian accent. His *jawohl* and their *jawohl* would have been laughable to a German.

Paul's life revolved around his identity as Army Intelligence agent. He liked the work and he liked the idea that he worked in clean clothes and no longer lived in foxholes expecting death or injury. He enjoyed Berlin and its bars and clubs. He drank too much, had trouble sleeping, and often dreamt of the dead Marine whose rifle he had taken to survive during the Battle of the Chosin Reservoir. He missed Marie and Buddy and he felt isolated from them and everyone else whom he considered "normal people." He often found himself in a rage and he had nowhere to direct it, so he drank even more.

He spent his nights drinking and reading books; books of all kinds from classics to trash. He studied the history of Berlin and the area of Germany now under Soviet control. He could recite the list of those who had ruled the area, the names of their leaders, the culture of Prussia, and other odd bits of this and that.

He spent time at the range firing every weapon he could get his hands on, from machineguns to handguns to specialized firearms disguised as other things. He practiced hand-to-hand combat and renewed his judo skills. He hated having time on his hands because it gave him time to think about his life and such reflection disturbed him and made him feel like a failure, someone whose only way to make a living was through violence.

He came to believe that the only people he really hated were the Koreans, the ones who had given him his worst moments. He referred to Koreans as "apes" and announced to anyone who would listen that the country would never rise to the level of a slum. The word "Korea" brought him the face of the dead Marine. He had seen many dead people, some gruesomely so, but this one was the face that haunted him.

By May the situation in East Berlin was explosive. The Soviets and their East German minions were raising taxes, cutting wages, raising quotas at factories, and making life even more miserable for the unfortunate Germans who found themselves in what was now being termed the "Eastern Bloc," those nation's dominated by Moscow.

The Soviets sent more tanks and troops into the streets in a show of force. Paul and the others in his unit were working full-time to gather intelligence about Soviet intentions. Other agents were in contact with East Germans who were trying to make life difficult for the Soviets by fomenting resentment and labor unrest.

Intelligence reports indicated that Walter Ulbricht, the Soviet puppet in charge of East Germany, had been called to Moscow and warned that if things got worse the result would be a catastrophe for him and his people. There was no need for the Soviets to be subtle or explicit. Everyone knew what they meant.

In mid June construction workers in East Germany went on strike. Western radio stations working with the American intelligence agencies offered the details of the strike and repeated calls for a general strike. The idea was fomented by American intelligence agencies. On June 17th thousands of East German workers marched on Berlin. East German security forces watched and did nothing, having received no orders from Moscow.

Paul was standing at the front of the House of Ministries when the rowdy crowd arrived and demanded the fall of the communist government. There was a scuffle between the thousands of angry workers and the few East German security forces at the building. He stayed to the side, not wanting to be caught up in whatever was going to happen. He took pictures with the Zorki and made mental notes about the makeup of the crowd. He recognized several East Germans who were working for the Americans. They were shouting anti-Soviet slogans.

Within an hour Soviet troops and tanks arrived to clear the area and the Soviets opened fire into the crowd. Security forces dragged protesters into vehicles and sped away. Paul was nicked by small pieces of stone from a building that was being hit by bullets. He watched as a middle-aged German was run over and crushed by a tank. He slipped behind a building to place a new roll of film in the Zorki when he heard screams and the sound of gunfire and saw bodies lying in the streets. He took more photos. A troop carrier loaded with Soviet soldiers sped in his direction and the officer in charge began shooting at him and shouting at his driver.

Paul ran for his life, down an alley and across several streets where security forces and angry workers were skirmishing. The Soviets had rallied their East German counterparts and an all-out struggle was underway. He heard the sound of gunfire behind him and a whistle, followed by orders for him to stop.

"Halt! Halt!" The Soviets were ordering everyone they saw to stop where they were. Everyone knew what falling into the hands of the Russians would mean; torture and death. The skirmishing continued and the crowd thinned as protesters were shot, captured, or ran away.

Paul managed to make it to the American sector by dark. His photographs didn't show anything that the world didn't already know. The Soviets were taking East Germany into a very dark period.

Chapter thirty

Flummery called a briefing on the morning after the massacre. He began by showing slides of the photos Paul had taken outside the House of Ministries. "This is what we know," he said, slamming his pointer into the screen. "What we don't know is what is happing to the poor people who were dragged away. We suspect that they're undergoing very harsh interrogation which will produce all kinds of confessions about their anti-Soviet and anti-socialist activities, then they'll be shot. The Soviets are cracking down all over their zone, taking over factories, sacking managers and local authorities, and vowing to shoot anyone who makes a move against them. We knew this was coming. The question now is what's next? That's where you come in. Headquarters needs to know what orders are coming from Moscow about troop movements and what it will mean for us. I don't have to tell you that general unrest in the East can mean bad trouble for the West. Questions?"

Paul raised his hand. "Do we have orders?"

"I'll get to that but the answer is yes."

Steve Wargo raised his hand. "Anything happening in Hungary?"

"Not yet. There's resentment over what the Soviets are doing but this bloodbath in Berlin might put a damper on plans there."

The question and answer session began to wander, as these things do, and when the questions degenerated to complaints about the quality of the coffee in the office kitchen, Flummery ended it.

"Brite, into my office."

Flummery turned up the music on the radio and handed Paul a folder. "I'd clean my weapons if I were you." He waved Paul to the door. "Tonight," he said, pointing to the folder.

Paul went to his desk and looked at his mission. It was simple. He was to break into Soviet military headquarters and steal, not photograph, any and all orders or classified material he could carry. The idea was to send a message to the Russians that the Americans were keeping an eye on them, something they already knew.

He would be going in alone but his driver would be accompanied by another man and both of them would be well armed and in position to come to his aid once he had grabbed the documents and other material.

Just as Berlin is dark for most of the day during the winter months, it is light for most of the day during the summer. The sun sets around nine in the evening in June and twilight can linger until ten. The sun is up well before five in the morning. Intelligence agents have a shorter window in which to perform their work. For those who labor in the dark arts, a dark night is an ally.

Paul's driver was waiting in the Soviet zone when he emerged from the apartment building that hid the tunnel. The driver was a young man, fit looking, wearing a Soviet uniform with the insignia of a sergeant. He was at the wheel of a Soviet jeep. A middle-aged man was in back. The man was wearing the insignia of a Soviet colonel, red strips on a gold background with gold stars. Both men wore the severe expression of Russian soldiers in the field. Neither man spoke.

Paul was wearing a cheap imitation leather jacket that had been made in East Germany. He was also wearing East German workman's boots. His jacket and his boots had been modified to hide the weapons he was carrying.

The man in the colonel's uniform handed Paul a sheaf of documents showing him to be a Norwegian observer. "This doesn't match the clothes," Paul said.

"Tell it to headquarters," the imitation colonel replied.

"No one will think I'm a diplomat. I'm dressed like the guy who fixes the toilet."

"I'm just the security man. You can call it off and complain or we can move ahead. Your call."

"Let's go."

Soviet checkpoints were well-manned and led by officers of at least the rank of major. Plain clothes men who reeked of KGB stood around and watched as people and vehicles were inspected.

The jeep was waved to the front of the line at the first checkpoint and the major in charge saluted the man he thought was a colonel and the vehicle proceeded. That was the case at two more checkpoints. At the fourth stop, the officer in charge was a colonel, so he ordered the jeep to stop so he could chat with his fellow officer. The man in back spoke fluent Russian and the two men chatted for several minutes. The Soviet officer did not ask for papers. They drove on.

"What did you two talk about," Paul asked.

"He wanted to know where I was from."

"What did you say?"

"After I found out he was from Leningrad, I told him I was from a village three time zones away. Russians from Leningrad think everyone from the sticks is an idiot and they attribute strange accents to ignorance of the mother language. He accepted that I was the Russian version of a hillbilly."

Paul smiled. "I know what you mean."

Headquarters had moved to a Soviet base closer to the center of Berlin. It was in a semi-rural area where there was room to marshal tank divisions, but it provided a location that was convenient for the crackdown in the city. Paul could see heavy security as they approached.

"This ain't gonna be easy," he said.

"If you can make it back to us we'll get you out," the driver said.

It was after midnight when Paul made it to the security fence. He heard barking dogs on the other side and was glad he was carrying a small bottle of Tobasco Sauce in case he had to run from them. He walked along the fence looking for breaks but the Soviets had taken care to ensure that the fence was in good repair. It was not electrified.

He cut through at a spot that wound through thick brush that had been cut back to allow for security vehicles to patrol. The brush would offer cover if someone came by. He made his way to edge of the trees and through the tanks and other vehicles that were lined up in a field. Several Soviet soldiers were on guard duty and he watched them for fifteen minutes to gauge their level of attention and whether they were being supervised. An officer marched down a row of tanks, shouted something at the guards, and returned to where he had come from. Once he was out of sight, the guard leaned against the tanks and smoked a cigarette.

There were no lights at the end of the formation and Paul moved between vehicles to a spot that offered a clear view of the headquarters building, which was busy with soldiers coming and going. The front of the building was guarded by soldiers whose Kalashnikovs were loaded.

He slowly made his way to a spot where he could view the back of the building and was relieved to see that it was unguarded and dark. He was nervous. There were people in the building. He had to get inside, find the correct office, open the safe or security drawer, grab the documents, and get out. He would need a diversion.

He went back to the tank formation and found a fuel depot where five gallon tanks were filled and stacked for their crews to pick up in the morning. Diesel fuel was for the tanks but gasoline was available for the other vehicles. He would need the gasoline. The fuel was guarded by a makeshift barbed wire fence whose gate was kept in place by a stick positioned through a slot where a padlock would go. The depot was illuminated by two light bulbs screwed into sockets that were strapped to wooden pole about twenty feet high. It had the look of something thrown together for the night.

One of the light bulbs was flickering on and off and Paul assumed it was about to burn out. It occurred to him that if he thought the light was about to go out, so did the Soviet soldiers. He found the power cord that fed electricity to the lights and followed it to a spot where it was plugged into a small generator. He checked the fuel level in the generator's tank and saw that it was almost empty. Another stroke of luck.

He pressed the fuel supply feed and the generator's engine quit. The lights went out. He hoped that the soldiers would take their time to investigate, assuming that the problem was bad bulbs or the generator's fuel, and not someone up to mischief.

He grabbed two of the five gallon fuel cans and moved halfway down a line of tanks. He could see that the guards were still at the far end, smoking and talking, and not paying attention. The guards would have been ordered to watch the woods and they would not be looking for trouble closer to the headquarters building.

He opened the fuel tanks and poured the gasoline over one of the tanks and under the one next to it. He poured a small line of the liquid to a spot between the rows and left the tanks in the middle of the gasoline. He took his Zippo out of his pocket and lit it, holding the flame down to the line, igniting it. He didn't wait for what happened next. He ran to a line of tanks about fifty feet away and then toward the headquarters building.

The five gallon containers exploded, ignited by the vapors trapped inside. The gasoline fire quickly spread to the two tanks. The fuel on the upper part of one tank caused it to light up the sky. The gasoline under the second tank heated up the diesel in its supply system and created a whoosing explosion that sent fire and parts showering onto the other vehicles.

Paul knew his opportunity would be short. He had to move in the shock and confusion that would quickly dissipate when experienced Soviet combat officers assessed the situation. The guards from the headquarters entranced stared at the fires and ran to investigate. Officers exited the building and joined the crowd watching the flames.

Paul picked the lock at the back door and made his way to the commander's office, which was easy to find because the general in charge was fond of the trappings of command. The general's safe was open and documents covered his desk. He had been working when Paul set things in motion.

He grabbed all of the documents, straightening them and shoving them into his jacket. He snapped a few photos of the office and walked into the hallway. A Soviet captain came out of the men's room and spotted him. For a moment, the two men stared at each other but the Soviet was first to pull his weapon, ordering Paul to place his hands on his head. The man spoke in German with a thick Russian accent and Paul shook his head and acted as though he didn't understand.

Paul held his hands up and looked confused. The Soviet experienced a moment of his own confusion and Paul held out his palm and said, *"ein Moment bitte,"* one moment please. He slowly reached into his shirt pocket and pulled out a cigarette with his thumb and forefinger. *"Zigarette."*

The Soviet frowned and pointed his handgun at Paul, motioning for him to raise his hands. Paul smiled and pointed to the cigarette. He reached into his front pocket. *"Feuerzeug."* Lighter.

The Russian opened his mouth to say something when Paul fired three rounds from the small Colt .25 caliber hammerless handgun in his pocket. One of the rounds hit the Soviet in the upper part of his leg. The other two slammed into his chest. The man stared at Paul, then at the blood coming through his blouse. Bloody foam dripped down his chin and he tried to cry out, making loud gurgling noises. Paul rushed to the man, took out his blackjack, and silenced the Russian with a blow to the back of his head.

He ran to the rear door, opened it to check for soldiers running to intercept him, and made his way to the line of tanks nearest the tree line. He was nearly at the fence when he heard the alarms and sound of shots being fired randomly in the confusion that follows the discovery of a body in a military headquarters building.

The guards who had been smoking at the rear of the formation were running in all directions and being yelled at by officers who were countermanding each other's orders. Paul heard the dogs barking and knew that they would be after him. He made it to the hole he had cut in the fence and took the Tobasco Sauce out of his jacket. He poured it over his shoes and rubbed it over his hands. He poured what was left on the ground at the hole and slipped through.

The Tobasco would interfere with the dog's ability to find his scent but it would only slow down the search, not end it. He ran to the meeting spot, dodging trees and brush, listening to the sounds of dogs howling. He knew they had found the Tobasco and were protesting the burn in their noses. He also heard shouting and gunfire and wondered what the Russians were shooting at. He used his flashlight to signal the security men and saw their jeep speeding to him.

"Climb in back and get under the tarp," the imitation colonel ordered. "I'm going to place some cargo on top of you. Don't move."

The first Soviet roadblock was manned by nervous soldiers under the command of a nervous young captain, who waved them through and yelled, "Good luck finding the jackal spies."

They made it back to Berlin before their papers were examined. The Soviets were not looking for enemies in Soviet uniforms and by dawn Paul was back in the American sector. By nine o'clock the Soviets had closed their checkpoints to the Western-controlled areas of the city.

Chapter thirty-one

Colonel Flummery called Paul to headquarters late in the afternoon. "Did you get some rest?"

"I was kind of wound up," Paul said.

"Let's go for a walk." Flummery pointed to the ceiling where, it was assumed, the Soviets were listening. The grounds of the old estate were being maintained by German laborers who, it was assumed, were likely to be on the Communist payroll. They were being supervised by American GIs who claimed some experience as gardeners. The result was a semi-elegant system of gardens with small ponds, lilies, roses and other plantings that were recent, given that Soviet tanks had destroyed the old gardens in the last days of the war.

Flummery and Paul walked in silence until they were well away from anyone else. "Two things," Flummery said. "First, great job. High command is very pleased. You're being promoted to Sergeant First Class. Congratulations." The promotion meant that Paul's base pay would jump to two-hundred-fourteen dollars per month, plus housing allowance. It was a thirteen dollar raise. At the time, no one in the Army, no matter how high up, made more than a thousand dollars per month.

"Thank you, Sir. It's welcome. My wife and I can use the money."

"Now to item number two. The Russians have filed a non-official protest claiming one of our agents killed an aide to their commanding general last night. It's non-

official because they don't want it to get out that one of
our agents got into their headquarters. That's how the
game is played. We'd probably do the same thing. Let's
hope we don't have to. At any rate, it's a safe bet that
they'll use their own assets to find out who was
responsible for the death of the captain and even the
score. You're being transferred immediately. You'll
pack your things and catch the evening train to
Frankfurt. You'll be working out of the I.G. Farben
Building. It's headquarters for a hell of lot of things and
you'll be around brass all day, but it's best to put you
somewhere safe."

"I'd like to stay in Berlin," Paul said.

"Not an option. You have orders. It's been a
pleasure." Flummery walked back to the mansion with
Paul behind him.

That night the Soviets stopped the train to Frankfurt
and examined the papers of everyone on board, even
those who claimed to be diplomats carrying protected
pouches. It was a harassment action not pinned to
anything in particular. The trains were supposed to
proceed between the Western sections of Berlin and
West Germany through an agreed-upon corridor that ran
through East Germany. The Soviets saw the corridor as
a means of showing their dislike for the West.

The Soviet officer who examined Paul's papers was
young and arrogant. He passed the papers to others to
examine and threatened to open Paul's luggage. "You
know, American, that spies are not protected under the
treaty that the Soviet Union generously signed as a
humanitarian gesture after the war. Are you a spy?"

"No, I'm just an observer," Paul replied.

"Did you fight in the war?"

"Yes, in the Army."

"Are you still in the Army?"

"Like I said, I'm an observer. Nothing more."

The Soviet officer tired of the game and moved on to another man. The train was stopped at a siding for four hours, prompting the Americans to issue a protest to the Soviet command, which ignored it.

He arrived at Frankfurt Bahnhof, which had been repaired after the war, and was busy when Paul stepped off the train at dawn. He was carrying a leather suitcase and a smaller bag called an "AWOL bag" by GIs because it was used by servicemen on weekend passes out of town. His orders were to report to the I.G. Farben building where he would see about finding quarters. He was tired. He had not slept after the killing of the Soviet captain and he had not slept on the train from Berlin.

He walked out of the Bahnhof's main entrance intending to find a taxi but a man was standing next to an Opel sedan, holding a photo and scanning the men leaving the station. He saw Paul and whistled.

"I'm your driver," he said by way of introduction. "The brass has you at Gutleut Kaserne. You'll be quartered there. I'm to get you settled in for the day and pick you up tomorrow morning at 0600."

"What's that, where you're taking me?"

"Gutleut Kaserne. Kaserne is German for barracks. It's actually a barracks complex. All kinds of units are there. The MPs have a whole battalion there. There's some intelligence and security stuff. Guys coming and going. Rumor has it that the SS used it during the war. It's old. Kind of medieval looking. You'll like it."

Gutleut Kaserne was not far from the Bahnhof and the driver drove through an archway and into a courtyard area, where he pulled up at doorway. "This is the orderly room for this place. Show them your orders."

Paul's orders were hidden under a cardboard cover in his suitcase. He had been travelling on false papers that would not get him a room in a U.S. Army barracks. The buck sergeant who was at the desk took one look at Paul and pegged him as a Military Intelligence type. Paul was wearing the kind of clothing the other MI troops were wearing and he looked like a GI checking in to a new assignment.

The sergeant waited for Paul to present his orders. He looked at them, found Paul's name on the register, and handed back the orders. "You're good, Sergeant. Your unit's billeted with the ASA. You're in the back and you guys have the fourth floor." ASA was the Army Security Agency, a signal intelligence unit that listened in to Soviet communications, among other duties. "You'll have a roommate but he's not here yet. He's coming in from Berlin in a few days."

"Do you have his name?" Paul asked.

The sergeant looked at his roster. "Staff Sergeant Steven Wargo. You know him?"

Paul smiled. "He's a friend."

"There's a mess hall at the rear of the complex. Regular GI food. There are lots of good German places within walking distance and the food and beer are out of this world and cheap." He handed a key to Paul. "I can get somebody to walk you up if you like."

"Is it hard to find?"

"Nope. Up the stairs to the fourth floor, hang a right, and walk down a long hall. You'll find it. Welcome to Frankfurt."

The city was nothing like Berlin, except for the Germans and the beer. Where Berlin has been tense and on edge, Frankfurt was relaxed and friendly. Where Berlin was at the center of the Cold War and was swarming with spies and counterspies, Frankfurt had no Soviet presence that was discernible and, while spies were in the city, they were not on every block; at least that was the assessment of those who concerned themselves with such things.

The I.G. Farben Building was the center of the American presence in West Germany. The Marshall Plan was run out of it. The Supreme Allied Command was in the building until 1952. The modern West German government was created there. Before the war it was a center of Nazi research, including the gas that was used in the concentration camps. Before the Nazis, it was headquarters of the I.G. Farben conglomerate and when the massive building was completed in 1930 it was the largest office building in Europe.

When Paul arrived it housed a long list of headquarters, agencies, and projects that were easy to hide in the building's six seven-story wings. It would require an entire division of Soviet spies to watch everyone entering and leaving.

There were no serious worries that the Soviets had bugged the place. The most secure rooms were swept regularly and radios were pointed at all of the windows in sensitive areas to block eavesdropping from the outside.

The MI unit was working out of a large room with standard-issue desks lined up along the walls and down the center. It looked like a big city newsroom of a large publication. Maps were displayed along the walls along with order of battle graphs for Soviet units.

The commanding officer of Paul's team was a major with an affected a British military bearing right down to the bushy mustache, the swagger stick, and tweed. His name was Malcolm Swink and his men saw him as a martinet. He had never heard a shot fired in anger, having spent the war in London reading intelligence reports and learning how to walk around with his hands behind his back in the British Royal manner. Paul disliked him at first sight.

Major Swink spent his days in a small office, reading and smoking a pipe. He toured his domain four times a day: in the morning when he arrived, when he left for lunch, when he returned from lunch, and when he pronounced his duty day was ended. He made exceptions to this schedule to welcome new men. He watched as Paul reported to the secretary who staffed the entrance to the room and was led to his desk.

"Hello. Sergeant Brite, is it?" he said in something approaching a British accent.

"Yes, Sir."

"Berlin, I'm told. Well done, chap."

Paul wasn't sure how to respond. "Yes, my last duty was in Berlin."

"You haven't seen the last of the old borderline city, not by any means." He caught Paul's blank reaction. "You aren't aware, are you? Berlin. It means borderline in German. You should brush up on your local culture. Comes in handy in our line of work." Swink had a self-satisfied smirk on his face as though he had caught one of the commoners being ignorant. "Well, Sergeant Brite, take a day or two to get the lay of the land and report to me for further instructions. Good day to you." At that, he placed his arms behind his back and marched back into his office where he lit his pipe and opened a German newspaper.

Paul thought Swink looked like a soft, doughy civilian. He tried to imaging the major surviving anything worse than a firecracker. Swink's feet were small and he walked with a girlish gait, making Paul snicker. He measured himself against a standard of survival under dire circumstances and Swink came up short in his estimation. It occurred to Paul that Swink probably spent his nights in deep, sweet sleep without the intrusion of the faces of dead men. That made him dislike the major even more.

Chapter thirty-two

Steve Wargo arrived two days later. He wore a black eye and walked with the aid of a cane. Paul was on his bunk reading when Wargo walked in dragging a canvas flight bag and an AWOL bag.

"What the hell happened to you?"

"Budapest happened. Things got kind of dicey with a Soviet border guard. Flummery thought it was a good idea to get me out of Berlin."

Paul knew that proper procedure required him to keep his questions to himself. Details of individual missions were shared only on a need-to-know basis and he had no need to know exactly how Wargo received his injuries.

"How you feeling?"

"Nothing a couple of aspirins and some good German beer won't fix."

"Lots of good places around here. The gasthauses are cheap and the food is good. We assume the other side takes our picture every time we go out, so it won't be long before our friends know we're here. Enough beer, and we'll invite them over to compare war stories." Gasthauses are to the Germans what pubs are to the English.

Paul sat up and admired Wargo's cane. The shaft looked like wood but up close it was clear that it was actually steel that had been made to look like wood. The handle was silver and ornate with indentations and carvings. "Nice. What's different about it?"

"It works as a cane but it's a shotgun," Wargo said. "The handle here unscrews and exposes the chamber. Insert a .20 gauge shell, screw the handle back on, and bingo! Loaded for action."

"How's the thing fire?"

"This decorative knob here pulls back. It's the firing pin. There's a small button here where my index finger rests when I'm holding the handle. Lift the cane, let it rest on the button, and stand back."

"Did you fire it?"

"Well, I'll say this. It came in handy."

"What kind of shells?"

"Kind of a specialized bird shot. It's designed for close in work. Within ten feet and it will pulverize anything it hits. At twenty feet you're on your own. The Soviets are in an uproar over what's happening in East Berlin and they're looking for guys like us. It helps to have a little firepower around."

"They won't try anything in Frankfurt. We just have to keep them from knowing when we're on their side of the fence. We're fair game over there."

"How're things in Berlin?"

"Pretty tight right now. The Soviets are keeping the lid on and they're rounding up a lot of good people. Some of them are ours. We're losing some good contacts. I'd bet we'll be going over to their side to recruit some new friends."

"Anything interesting happening in your area?"

Paul was sending out an open question about Hungary that Wargo could answer or bat away.

"The Soviets are just as nasty in Hungary. Life is hard and the people have no love for the Russians. Hungarians are proud people and they feel about the Bolsheviks the way they felt about the Nazis. Basically, get the hell out. That's how they feel. Fertile ground for us."

Major Swink did not have a tactical mind. He was an analyst and felt comfortable at his desk, looking over reports. He liked living in a small world and smoking his pipe while he read about things that other people did. He was not comfortable around field agents like Paul and Wargo and several others who had been pushed on him by Berlin. He was unhappy when he received a dispatch informing him that Paul and Wargo would remain under the command of Colonel Flummery and he was to confine his role to providing desks and other administrative support.

Paul and Wargo spent their days reading reports about what was happening in the Soviet-controlled areas of Germany and Hungary. Others were reading about Poland, Czechoslovakia, Latvia and other captive nations. The primary concern was Soviet intentions vis-à-vis West Germany and whether a Warsaw Pact invasion was likely or even possible. It was assumed that if the Soviets moved against the West they would do it with large contributions from the nations they were currently repressing. Western analysts saw this as a point for their side.

Marshall Law had been declared in the Soviet-controlled areas of Berlin and throughout East Germany to prevent what the East German Politburo referred to as "the intrusion of fascist bandits from West Berlin."

Paul liked the phrase so much he hand wrote a sign and taped it to the front of his desk. It read, "Fascist bandit. Inquire within."

Wargo added a sign to his desk that read, "Hungarian fascist bandit. Call for rates."

Colonel Flummery got the last laugh. He sent a dispatch to both men. It was short. "Night train to Berlin in all haste."

Both men were on the train that night and were searched by Soviet border guards who examined their papers and moved on. The guards were more interested in an Army captain who was carrying a briefcase handcuffed to his wrist. The captain pulled out an Army .45 and warned the Soviets to move on. There was a short staring match and the Soviets exited the train and it went on to Berlin, where Flummery was waiting with a car.

Paul looked out the window as the driver navigated the streets of Berlin. It was a gray morning and the city was depressing. Military police jeeps were everywhere and checkpoints were tense. The Soviets had their side all but locked down and the sounds of gunfire could be heard in the morning air. Frankfurt was free and open. Berlin was like a prison. The solemn hatred and vengeance that the Soviets had imposed in their sector seemed to float like a gas over the western part of the city, even as men and women sat at outdoor cafes and downed their morning coffee and pastries. *Well, at least they have coffee and sweets*, Paul thought. *The poor bastards on the other side are making do with weak tea and stale brown bread.*

Flummery was in no mood to make jokes to the assumed microphones in the ceiling. He took Paul and Wargo into his office and turned up the radio to an ear-splitting level and called the two men to him. "Here are your folders. Take them upstairs and read them. You'll be recruiting some replacements for us. We have already made the contacts. You just have to set up the signals and systems." With that he waved at the door and the two men left.

Paul's assignment was a man who was a supervisor at a machine shop in Pankow, a suburb where many of the new East German bureaucrats were living. The man had been an officer in the Wehrmacht and had surrendered to the Americans in Bavaria, but he had come home to see to his family and was being detained by the Soviets as a war criminal in need of "reeducation."

He was a chemist by training and had been drafted into the German army after serving as a conscript in one of I.G. Farben's chemical facilities. The Soviets alleged that in addition to his service in Hitler's army he had taken part in ghastly Nazi research. He and his family were living in dire conditions with the constant threat of deportation to a labor camp. The man was, therefore, an ideal candidate to work for the Americans.

A meeting had been arranged in the man's home for the following night. Paul's job would be to talk with the man and assess his sincerity and if he was satisfied to establish a system of exchanging information and payment. He would be paid in DDR marks, which were worthless in the West. He would be paid the equivalent of fifty dollars a month, a fortune on the Soviet side. Whether the man was smart enough to hide his wealth was a concern but not something that would keep Paul up nights. It was up to the German to save himself.

Paul was driven to Pankow in an Opel that had seen better days. His papers identified him as a Swiss observer who was part of the international effort to monitor what was happening in East Germany. The Kremlin felt that it was better to allow a few so-called observers in to look around than endure the endless bloody headlines that were being splashed across the world's newspapers.

Paul's driver was a Swiss citizen who spoke German and French, along with a smattering of Russian. The man had been a Swiss guard at the Vatican in the late forties and was working for Western intelligence out of religious outrage. He had also been trained to defend himself and the Pope and was therefore no milquetoast.

Paul's target lived above the shop on a street that had yet to see the post war cleanup that the Soviets were promising. Some of the buildings were rubble from bombs or artillery. Others bore pockmarks of the fighting that had raged there in the last days of the war.

The name Paul would to use to address the man was Kurt Ahler. His real name would remain hidden in the event that the Soviets got their hands on Flummery's agent list. Ahler was nearing forty. He had been married since 1941. He had two children, both born after the war.

Ahler opened the door with a look of panic and fear. He motioned for Paul and the driver to come in and quickly closed the door and pulled the curtain's shut.

"Guten Abend!" Paul said. Good evening.

"I speak English," Ahler replied. "So does my wife." The woman stood at a dining table wringing her hands and looking worried.

"This won't take long. May we sit?"

Paul made small talk for a few minutes, commenting on the weather and the roads. Ahler seemed to be having trouble catching his breath.

"Do you know what will be required of you?" Paul asked, looking at the man and his wife.

"Yes, I believe so." Ahler looked at his wife, who nodded.

"You and I or possibly someone else from our side would meet from time to time to exchange information. I believe you know or have contact with DDR officials who live near here and you do work for them. Is that correct?"

Ahler and his wife nodded.

"There are Soviet military units in the area. We would be interested in any information about them such as unit rotations, troop movements, and so on."

Again, Ahler and his wife nodded.

"Do you have anything for me tonight?"

Ahler took a deep breath and stood up. His wife followed him to a cupboard where he removed a small, leather-covered box. Such a box was a common storage place for tobacco and rolling papers. Both were in short supply in East Germany. The man opened the box and removed a piece of folded paper, which he handed to Paul.

"These are the names of DDR officials who live near me. I have added the license plate numbers of their cars and their addresses, along with what I know about them. Most are functionaries and do not make policy but they are charged with carrying out policy. And like everywhere else, we have tank units in the fields beyond the town. I will get you their designations." Ahler's hands were shaking.

Paul took the paper, read it, and crumpled it up and put it in his shoe. He would remember what was on it long enough to dictate the names and other information. He would discard the paper if it became necessary. He stood up and shook hands with Ahler and his wife and handed the man ten five-mark notes. "One week from tonight we will return. If there is a problem you are to put the box in the window. If we have a problem we simply will not show up and in that event we will schedule for one week after that. Are we clear?"

Ahler and his wife looked relieved when Paul and his driver walked to the door. "*Danke*." Thank you.

Paul was in Flummery's office at daylight, dictating what was on the paper. Flummery looked at the list and nodded. "Good work. Now you need to get back to Frankfurt. We don't want you spending too much time in Berlin. I got you a MATS flight out of Tempelhof. It leaves at nine. I'll get you a ride."

"What about Wargo?"

"He's not back yet. Let's leave it at that."

Tempelhof Airport was the main entry point for American Air Force planes that were vital to supply and man the U.S. military in Berlin. The Soviets harassed incoming and outgoing flights but didn't shoot them down, so the Air Force pilots became used to the challenges of flying to Berlin. The Military Air

Transport Service, MATS, was a passenger and troop transport system that ran regular runs from Berlin to Frankfurt and other locations in West Germany. Some of the aircraft were passenger planes and others were cargo planes that hauled troops and supplies.

Paul hated to fly. It was a fear that he never got over. He was tense and worried about dying in a crash from liftoff to landing. He found himself board a C-47 that was hauling freight to Frankfurt. The flight should have taken less than an hour but the Soviet harassment slowed flight time and it was nearly two hours before the aircraft set down at Rhein-Main Air Force Base, which shared space with the international airport at Frankfurt. Rhein-Main was billed by the U.S. Military as the "gateway to Europe" and cargo, passenger, and fighter aircraft were landing and taking off at all hours.

The C-47 pulled into a spot on the tarmac and the engines shut down. The crew chief, an Air Force sergeant, removed his headphones and tapped Paul. "This is where you get off. There's the terminal over there." He pointed to a building about two hundred yards away. "Maybe they can get you a ride." He turned to the task of unloading the cargo.

A jeep and driver were waiting for Paul and he was at his desk in the I.G. Farben Building by noon.

Swink was in full British regalia, complete with hunting cap. "How was your little trip?"

"It was fine, Sir. Colonel Flummery sends his regards."

"Yes, of course. Carry on." Swink's small feet carried him out the door to his lunch.

"Twinkle Toes," Paul muttered.

A pattern had been established. Paul made short trips to Berlin to meet with newly recruited agents on the other side and then caught a flight back to Frankfurt. Wargo's trips were longer and Paul assumed he was travelling to Hungary, but Wargo's trips were never discussed and neither were Paul's.

Chapter thirty-three

In October, with the German winter looming, Major Swink swapped his ersatz British linen suits for Scottish tweed. He sucked on his pipe and paced the office, hands behind his back, observing his men, most of whom thought he was a fool.

"Carry on, men. That's the lad. Hip, hip and all that."

Paul watched Swink and wondered how such a man could become a major. How he had become an officer was mystery. *Maybe he has qualities that are not evident to us*, Paul thought. *Or maybe he just knows the right asses to kiss.*

"Brite, ah yes, just the man I was hoping to find." Swink had a smile on his face.

Paul thought the comment was ridiculous. How could Swink not find him? "Yes, Sir."

"Got some paperwork here. Your request to have your family join you has been approved. You'll be required, as you know, to extend for at least three years after they arrive, which, according to what I've seen, should be shortly before Christmas. You'll be assigned quarters adequate to your needs and whatever else the U.S. and German governments provide." He handed some papers to Paul. "It's all here."

Paul was elated. Marie and Buddy would be joining him and they would live together as a family for at least three years and maybe more. The cost of living was low.

Travel around Europe was easy. He sat back and allowed himself a moment to savor.

In December Marie and Buddy boarded the U.S.S. Shanks for a seven-day crossing of the North Atlantic. The Shanks was a troop ship that had been fitted with cabins for dependent families. The crossing was rough with high seas rolling the ship front to back and side to side. Dependents were feted in the dining room three times a day with white table cloth, silver service, and better-than-average Navy food served by Filipino waiters in white jackets.

Two days out and most of the passengers were too seasick to dine. The troops in the hold were being fed Army chow of the watery stew variety in close quarters at the bottom of the ship, which was rolling night and day. The outdoor areas were off limits because of the high seas. The air in the cabins and dining hall smelled of vomit. The Filipino waiters wet down the tablecloths to keep the plates from sliding onto the floor.

Marie could not eat. She took to her bed and kept a wet towel on her forehead, and moaned for Buddy to leave her alone. She had nothing left to expel and still she felt miserable. "I can't take this. If I could get off I would."

Buddy was not affected by the rolling of the ship. In fact, he thought it was wonderful. He went up to the recreation room, which looked out over the bow of the ship, and watched the waves crash over the railings. He went to the dining room for all meals and joined the half-dozen other passengers who were well enough to eat, consuming eggs, bacon, soup, steaks, cakes and anything else that was put in front of him. He liked watching the tableware slide around while he enjoyed his meal.

Each table had a large bowl of fresh fruit as a centerpiece. He stuffed his pockets with apples, oranges and pears and snuck down to the troop level where he traded the fruit for a space on the floor to watch movies with the soldiers. The smells of vomit and sweat didn't bother him. He made the mistake of telling his mother where he went and she forbade him from going down to the hold. "Those are rough men. It's no place for a boy."

He responded by keeping secret his time out of the cabin. He was ten years old and had free rein on an ocean-going vessel. He ate, played, watched movies with the troops, watched movies with other kids in the dependents theater, played chess in the recreation room, and had the time of his life, all while most of the adults were barely able to get through the day.

The Shanks entered the English Channel and the seas calmed enough for the captain to allow passengers to stand at the rails and get some fresh air. Marie and Paul gazed at the white cliffs of Dover and Marie sang in a French accent:

There'll be blue birds over
The white cliffs of Dover,
Tomorrow ,just you wait and see.
There'll be love and laughter
And peace ever after
Tomorrow, when the world is free.

She had tears in her eyes as she sang the song that helped get the British through the war. It was a sentimental moment that brought her the sadness and worry she had lived with while Paul was away fighting. "We're finally going to be a family," she said.

A few days before Christmas the Shanks docked in Bremerhaven and the dependents gratefully departed, many of them vowing never to travel by ship again. There was an overnight train to Frankfurt in sleeper cars. The women slept and the children looked out the window and wished they could see Germany. All they saw were lights.

On a cold, gray morning, the train pulled into the Bahnhof to the anxious looks of soldiers in uniform, most of them holding flowers. Paul was in the crowd, pacing and smoking and wondering if Marie would like Germany well enough to stay for three or four years. Marie and Paul exited the train dragging heavy suitcases down a concrete platform in a crowd of American women and children. Buddy saw Paul first and yelled.

The Army put everyone up at a German resort in the country while quarters were made ready. On December 20th, the Brites moved into an apartment building on Adickesalle in a half-bombed out area of Frankfurt. The street was lined with pre-war buildings that had mostly escaped the bombing, but nearby streets were not as fortunate and many of the buildings were still ruins waiting for attention.

Their apartment was on the third floor and was, by most standards, charming. It was furnished with Germany products, including hand-blown crystal and high quality china. All of it courtesy of the German government as part of its reparations.

On a snowy, and for Buddy, magical night, he and Paul set out to find a Christmas tree. It was Christmas

Eve and the pickings were slim. The Germans did not have the luxury of tree farms in those years. They were still consumed with the business of staying alive and finding enough food. A single tree remained at a corner stand and a middle-aged German man was standing at attention next to it. Paul and Buddy walked up and the man bowed to Paul and shook Buddy's hand. He then pointed to the tree and held up three fingers. The price of the tree was three marks. At the time, one mark equaled twenty-five cents. Paul handed the money to the man, whose eyes misted over.

The tree was very ugly and spare of branches. It had no discernible Christmas tree shape. It was more like a stick with evergreen needles. Paul and Buddy carried it to their new apartment, stopping at a small store to purchase a few ornaments and a string of lights. They set up the tree and decorated it. Snow was falling outside, Armed Forces Radio Frankfurt was playing Christmas carols, and Buddy was as happy as he had ever been.

"It's magic here," he said.

Marie's eyes teared up and she held Paul's hand. "We're going to like it here."

Paul couldn't speak. He tried to come to terms with the moment. Part of him couldn't believe that his life had produced it. He had lived on a diet of violence all of his life. Love had come to him by the tiniest of measures. He was terrified that it was a dream or worse, that he would do something to destroy it.

Outside, in the German night, men like him were observing each other with malice. They were armed and lethal. One death was no different than another. There was no magic in the night for these men.

Inside the apartment, the very air was magic in the glow of the lights on the small, ugly tree. Marie went to the window and watched as the snow covered the street. Men and women rode bicycles along the bike paths that had been placed between the sidewalk and the street. Lowell seemed very far away and she was grateful that she was no longer there. She folded her hands and closed her eyes and crossed herself.

L'ange de Dieu, mon gardien cher
À qui l'amour de Dieu me commet ici
Jamais la nuit être à mon côté
Allumer et garder, gouverner et guider. Sont
Angel of God, my guardian dear
To whom God's love commits me here
Ever this night be at my side
To light and guard, to rule and guide.
Amen.

Paul watched her pray and wondered at the mystery of faith. *Maybe God has no place for warriors.* He looked at his wife and felt a vast distance between them. In his mind she was good and pure and innocent. He saw himself as stained and unworthy. He had seen and done too much for God to pay him any respect.

"I have some champagne," he announced. He opened a bottle to great fanfare and poured three glasses. Buddy thought it was awful, but he drank enough to make him sleepy. Paul carried the boy to his new room and closed the door. He and Marie celebrated their reunion with vows to make it work.

Chapter thirty-four

Buddy was ten. He had spent less than three years with his father, whom he didn't know in a serious way. A few months here and there is not the same as day-to-day living in what most people would define as a normal life. Soldiers do not live normal lives and neither do their families. Paul set out to get to know his son.

Most days, Paul went to work in the morning and came home at night. He was away several days each month and everyone in the family knew that what Paul did was not to be spoken of. Paul and Marie developed a circle of friends whose lives were similar. Spies whose friends were spies and wives of spies.

Evenings were homework for Buddy, reading for Marie, and training for Paul. He would sit on the sofa with a satchel full of locks, close his eyes, and use his locking picking tools to open them, timing himself. He practiced with both hands and with one hand, left or right. He taught Buddy how to clean weapons by taking them apart, wiping away residue and rust, and oiling them. He instructed him on gun safety. He taught him how to use the sights for longer range firing and how to shoot in close quarters by aiming from the hip. He taught him how to sharpen a knife. How to use a blackjack. How to throw someone who's bigger and stronger.

Buddy never thought it was unusual to spend his evenings like this and, in fact, assumed that his friends spent their evenings learning the fine art of violence with their dads, although no one ever talked about it because they didn't talk about anything associated with their fathers.

One day Paul came home with a cane. He had a gleam in his eye as he showed it to Marie, who wasn't impressed.

"Don't keep it loaded," she said. "We have enough guns around here."

"I'm goin' to teach Buddy how to shoot it," Paul said.

"Don't do anything stupid." Marie had not grown up around guns and the only violence she had experienced as a girl was the yelling that erupted between her siblings.

The Military Intelligence gun range was located in a semi-rural area a few miles outside Frankfurt. It had the usual known-distance firing lines but it also offered other opportunities for the agents to practice their craft through windows, doors, plywood alleys, rooms, and woods. Most of the agents were happy to spend a few hours a week firing whatever they could get their hands on. The weapons were interesting and the ammo was free. Handguns, assault rifles, specialized weapons, firearms from the Eastern Bloc, it was all there. And a shotgun that looked like a decorative cane.

"Follow me, "Paul said, heading down a path through the woods. He took Buddy to a clearing where a downed log was set against a small hill. There were cases of Coke bottles nearby and Paul set a half-dozen of them on the log.

"Watch this," he said. He loaded a shell into the cane, screwed the handle back on, pulled back the ornate firing pin, raised the cane, and fired. The first Coke bottle turned to dust. "Damn!" he said. "Let's do it again."

Buddy was fascinated and eagerly waited for each round to pulverize the target bottle. Paul went through about a dozen before he turned to Buddy with a smile on his face. "Your turn."

The bottles were about ten feet away and Buddy missed on his first shot. Paul was patient and reloaded. Buddy hit the second bottle but not square on, knocking it off the log but not turning it to dust. By his fifth shot he had the idea and when the two cases were gone Paul and Buddy were congratulating themselves on their marksmanship with the cane.

"Pretty good shooting," Paul said. "I'd say you're a natural. We have to get you out here again and do something with real handguns. How'd you like to learn to shoot a Lugar?"

For his second Christmas in Germany Buddy was given a set of throwing knives. Six months later he could stick a knife in a board from twenty feet. He could shoot handguns, an M1, a shotgun, a cane, and he knew the basics of knife fighting.

He also played baseball, knew the secret tunnels of his neighborhood, rummaged through bombed-out buildings, and had a few run-ins with German boys whose parents had taught them to despise Americans.

He learned the social code among the Americans who were in the business of secrets. The kids whose dads worked for the CIA said their fathers worked for the State Department. The kids whose fathers worked in

Military Intelligence said they didn't know what their fathers did.

Two years into their German life, the Brites moved to a new housing complex that had been built for the American dependents. All of the intelligence families lived in the same cluster of three-story apartment buildings, regardless of rank up to a point. All of the dads wore civilian clothing so rank was not on display when they went to work and came home.

To his dismay, Paul discovered that Major Swink had been assigned quarters in the same building where he, Marie and Buddy were to live. It had been ordered that the two men not acknowledge each other when they were not on duty. This was not out of military courtesy or protocol but out of concern that Soviet agents, who were assumed to be infesting the new housing area, would link the men and others and create an organizational chart that would help them keep track of American agents.

Paul thought it was preposterous. "Hell, they already know who we are. The only secret we have to keep from them is where we are and what we're doing." He stood at the front window of the apartment and watched as Swink walked to his car in the morning, mumbling, "Swink" under his breath. On several occasions he turned to Marie and said, "That man is as bad as a civilian."

The Soviets and their Warsaw Pact allies liked to rattle their sabers and feint at the border with West Germany. Under the cover of maneuvers they would mass troops and tanks near the border and announce war games. The Western powers had no choice but to assume that part of the game was to assess how NATO would respond. Alerts were common. Even dependents would be placed on alert status, ready to evacuate should the Soviets storm west.

Phone calls would go out in the middle of the night and Marie and Paul and thousands of other women and children would grab pre-packed suitcases and ride busses to marshaling points in drills that were as serious as those the soldiers were experiencing. Buddy and his friends learned to see the drills as games, sort of like fire drills at school.

The Military Intelligence and Army Security Agency units in Germany were tasked with keeping eyes and ears on the Soviets and assessing their intentions. West Germany was twice as large at East Germany. The southern half of West Germany bordered Czechoslovakia. The area where West and East Germany met Czechoslovakia was well guarded by both sides. Fences, walls, mine fields, guard towers and military stations dotted the border. It was seen as a potential flash point.

On the West German side, bucolic hills and woods were bisected by streams. It was the perfect place to find peace and solace in a troubled world. The problem for Paul was how to get close enough to see what was happening on the other side without drawing too much attention to himself. The Soviets had been known to take shots at people on the West side for small provocations. He decided that he needed a good cover as a diversion and he believed that Buddy was the answer.

In the late spring of 1955, Paul, Wargo and Buddy set out from Frankfurt in the hours before dawn to drive down to the area for a fishing trip. Paul woke Buddy in the still-dark hours, made him a breakfast of scrambled eggs and bacon, and drove to pick up Wargo, who was living in the complex with the other MI types and their families.

By dawn they were walking along a trout stream that trickled down a gentle slope toward an open valley, the other side of which was marked by a tall fence and guard towers. On the hillside, the stream was lined with trees and other vegetation that had been cleared through the valley to allow better observation of what was happening at the border. Paul and Wargo wore P38s in holsters on their belts. Each man carried a Leica C3 camera and Leitz binoculars. Paul's Leica was equipped with a long lens.

"Why are you carrying guns?" Buddy asked.

"Snakes," Paul said. "There might be snakes around here."

"Are they poisonous?"

"I don't think so. But there are a couple of adders in Germany. I wouldn't worry about being bitten if I were you. If you see one, let us know."

Paul stayed with Buddy while Wargo went off on his own. He was gone about an hour and came back in a hurry. "Maybe we should find another spot," he said. Half an hour later the three were working another stream that overlooked the border. This time Wargo stayed with Buddy while Paul went off on his own.

They managed to catch two trout and were back home by early afternoon.

Chapter thirty-five

Paul was as happy as he had ever been. His life was, for the most part, settled, even though his way of making a living was not in the mainstream. He travelled to Berlin, went on his missions, took Buddy on fishing trips to the border areas, and strengthened his marriage to Marie.

They travelled throughout Europe, visiting Paris, Brussels, Amsterdam, Luxembourg and cities in West Germany. They stayed in grand hotels and toured castles and cathedrals. They took Buddy to the great museums and explained why the art on display was cherished by generations.

Paul's face softened and he laughed more. His friends in MI became an extended family and they all picnicked together in the parks, renting row boats and enjoying a life that would have been unimaginable to them during the war years or the Depression.

The reality of the Cold War came crashing into their lives in October of 1956 when the Hungarian people, fed up with the brutal Soviet occupation, rose up across the country and demanded that the Soviet troops leave. The Kremlin would have none of it and slammed the hammer down after feigning a willingness to withdraw its force.

The Warsaw Pact went on alert and thousands of troops and tanks were on the move. NATO needed information about Soviet intentions and the ever-present threat of a move against the West.

Colonel Flummery's agents were brought to Berlin and briefed. They then headed east. Wargo went to Budapest with two sets of papers, one to get him into the country, the second to get him out. Paul went into East Berlin, met his driver, and went to the Polish border to gather intelligence about Soviet units that were moving.

The logical route to Hungary is through Austria where there's a border. The Americans knew it and so did the Soviets. In fact, spies were going both ways through the border there but some of it was just intelligence noise to keep border guards occupied. Wargo went through Czechoslovakia, where internal controls were looser than in East Germany or, now that an uprising was underway, in Hungary. Still, the Czech's were on edge because their Soviet masters were looking over their shoulders. Wargo had a few tense moments as his papers were being scrutinized but his Hungarian was fluent and without accent and he was allowed movement.

Paul's papers again identified him as a Swiss observer and a member of the Swiss Communist Labour Party, a far-left group numbering some twenty-thousand that agitated for social fairness in Switzerland. Swiss Communists were often at odds with each other over Soviet policies in Eastern Europe and observers were a common sight in Soviet-controlled areas, often eagerly lapping up whatever propaganda the Soviets threw their way. Many Soviet authorities referred to the Swiss Communists as "spaniels" and saw them as harmless creatures to be assured that all was well. Paul's papers got him through many checkpoints with a wave and a smile.

Paul was looking for evidence of Soviet movement. The Kremlin's military doctrine was based on the idea that war was simply another means of achieving the expected victory of socialism over capitalism. Moscow's military leadership believed that success was inevitable and resistance was futile. The Soviet generals also believed in attacking in unexpected ways and places with overwhelming force and violence.

Movement of forces to the West toward Berlin or even West Germany would present a very different scenario than movement of forces toward Hungary.

He saw lines of tanks on the roads and that told him the Soviets were moving, but they were going in all directions. He assumed they knew men like him were observing them and were feinting here and there.

It was autumn and sunny and he enjoyed the ride. The game of cloak and dagger made him feel alive. He watched the tanks and armored troop carriers with the same eye a tourist might gaze upon windmills or charming small farms. This was how things were in the world. He briefly thought that Buddy would enjoy the show and went over in his mind how he would explain the formations and vehicles. "The Soviets have what are called tank armies. The tank armies have two to four armored divisions plus motorized rifle, artillery, intelligence, and other divisions." Buddy would nod and understand and admire his father's knowledge.

The lethality of what he was observing was lost in his reverie, no more important than a bull fighter admiring an animal. Men like Paul have nothing in common with men in offices in far away, peaceful cities.

Office politics are kindergarten games compared with the assessment of the intentions of Warsaw Pact divisions. He liked the idea of firepower, muzzle velocity, tactics, and the applied use of violence. It had been the signature of his adult life. He kept his weapons cleaned, his knife sharp, his senses on alert.

His driver was a former Wehrmacht captain and a native of East Germany. He was a card-carrying member of the Communist Party and an informer for the Stasi, the DDR secret police. His name was Rudolph Sansinger and he was the political equivalent of a sociopath. He had no loyalties and therefore he was available on the open market. On this day he would be in the service of Paul and the West. In coming days he would duly report all that he had done with Paul and how it had been arranged. In a month or two the process would be reversed and he would offer information about how his reports concerning Paul had been received and what, if any, action had been taken. There were many Rudolph Sansingers in the game.

He turned onto a side road that was nothing more than two parallel dirt paths cutting across a field and into a forest. The car pulled to a stop in a grove of trees that had lost most of their leaves. Sansinger turned to Paul and said in English, "One hour."

Paul got out carrying the cane. He slipped a small pebble into his shoe to make him limp and he set out down the dirt path toward the sound of diesel engines in the distance. Ten minutes later he was at tall security fence with warning signs facing out. The fence was topped with rolled barbed wire and porcelain insulators on the tops of the concrete posts told him the fence was electrified. The Soviets were not hesitant to run lethal loads through their security fencing. There was no sound coming from the fence to tell him that it was hot, so he picked up a handful of wet soil and threw it as the fence to see if sparks came off. There was nothing to indicate the power was on. He touched it with a wet stick and still there were no sparks. For reasons known only to the Soviets, the power to the fence was off. That could change at any time.

He quickly touched it with his hand and it was cold and inactive. Using wire cutters, he made a hole in the fence and marked the spot on both sides with downed branches pointing in and out. He was through and in the cover of trees within seconds and removed the pebble from his shoe to give him speed.

He moved to the sound of the tank engines and found himself at the edge of what appeared to be a headquarters area where squad tents were set up in a wide circle around what to Paul looked like a field office. He knelt and took out his Zorki camera, snapping photos with a long lens. He could either stay where he was and map the headquarters, or he could move away to a spot where he could observe the formation of the tanks and count them.

He heard the sound of leaves being crushed and turned to look into the face of a man wearing the insignia of a Soviet Major General. The man stared at him and appeared to be trying to place him. Paul turned, stood, and snapped a photo of the man. As the general was backing up and reaching for his sidearm, Paul charged and jammed the tip of the cane into the man's throat. The general's eyes bugged out as he gagged and fell back, managing a gargled shout that alerted others in the camp.

Paul silenced the general with the blackjack and reached into the general's coat hoping to find his identification papers. He discovered a wad of documents and other papers in the man's breast pocket, grabbed them, and ran into the woods as shouts and orders were erupting behind him. He could hear men coming to the general and the confusion over what had happened to the man. The confusion gave Paul time to reach the hole in the fence before he turned to see a Soviet enlisted man running at him, aiming his Kalashnikov.

Paul dropped into a prone position and removed the tip of the cane, which both protected the barrel and acted as tweezers to extract the spent shotgun shell. He aimed the cane at the soldier and fired, sending a burst of birdshot into the man and creating a red cloud where the Soviet had been aiming his rifle. The soldier went down screaming. Paul ran down the path and found Rudolph Sinsinger waiting with the engine running.

It took the Soviets over an hour to respond en masse and by that time Paul was on a train bound for East Berlin. His papers had got him past the loose security that was unaware of the pandemonium at the tank division's headquarters.

Halfway to Berlin the train was stopped by Soviet security personnel and a search was begun. Every male passenger was forced from the train and ordered to stand at attention while the Soviets searched the train and all of the baggage. They dumped the contents of suitcases where they were and poked the seats with bayonets. They went down the line of men, demanding identification papers and asking questions. Some of the men who fit the description of the man who attacked the general were singled out and beaten with batons.

227

Two Soviet security troops came to Paul and held out their hands for his papers. He fumbled and looked confused, leaning forward and asking in German, *was?* What?

The Soviets were impatient and the one who appeared to be in charge motioned for Paul to turn over his documents. *"Papiere. Jetzt."* Papers. Now.

Paul cowed like a man fearing a beating, reached into his coat pocket, and handed the Soviet a large wad of documents that contained his identification, old newspaper clippings, the train schedule, a German to Russian dictionary, and, in the middle, the documents he had seized from the general. *"Meine Papiere sind herein dort."* My papers are in there. He stooped and looked fearful.

The Soviet took the papers and held them for a moment. He looked up at Paul and slapped him with the wad of documents and threw them to the ground and stormed off to the next man. Paul picked them up and shyly put them back in his pocket. The Soviet had held the documents that were the object of the search and had received them from the man they were looking for, but his impatience and arrogance had blinded him to the idea that the general's precious documents were hiding in his own hands.

By midnight Colonel Flummery and his analysts had identified the general and were reading his orders from Moscow.

The 1960's

Chapter thirty-six

"When a man is in despair, it means that he still believes in something."
Dmitri Shostakovich

By the mid 60s Paul was riding a desk at the headquarters of the Army Security Agency in Arlington, Virginia, reading reports, clipping newspapers, and thinking about retirement. He was in his mid 40s and had been a soldier since before the Second World War. Marie was constantly reminding him that there was more to life than the Army. Buddy was on his own, having put in a hitch as a paratrooper in an ASA unit.

Paul was middle aged and happy. His job wasn't particularly challenging but it wasn't dangerous, either. Old spies sit at desks and read the work of young spies. He had gained weight and had, for the first time in his life, a "bit of a tummy," as Marie put it. He rode to work in a carpool with other middle-aged soldiers whose dangerous days were behind them. He drank less, slept better, and grew tomatoes and cantaloupes in his back yard. His neighbors knew him as that nice soldier.

He wore a uniform to work and neglected to wear his ribbons, preferring only his Combat Infantry Badge with star, signifying combat in two wars. His commanding officer ordered him to wear his ribbons as part of his uniform but he chose to wear only those that related to his war time service, ignoring the ones he termed "good boy" ribbons for good conduct and other non-combat achievements.

He was a Master Sergeant. He wanted to retire as a Sergeant Major, the highest enlisted rank. It would mean more money in retirement and to him it meant even more. It was a matter of pride. He wanted to prove to himself and the Army that he was as good as any man. He was no stranger to the politics of rank and he learned that a Sergeant Major slot would open in about a year. There were two clear front runners, Paul and another Master Sergeant who had also seen combat and had an outstanding record in Intelligence. Word came through unofficial channels. The slot would go to the man who would volunteer to spend a year as a combat intelligence briefer working out of the ASA station at Phu Bai, Vietnam.

Paul stepped forward. The other man put in his retirement papers. Marie was furious. "He's the one with the good sense," she said. "The other guy isn't going to put his wife through another damned war. He's not going to put her through that. Damn you!" Marie was teary and on the verge of hysteria. "How much money are we talking about? A few more dollars a month? Let the young guys go over there, Paul."

"It's only a year, not like the other times. I'm not in a combat unit. I'll be sacked out most of the time, reading magazines." He wasn't convincing.

A week before he departed he called Buddy to go with him to a gun shop in Virginia. "I need you to help me with something."

They met for dinner and Paul looked across the table. "I need you to look after your mother. I'd like you to move in with her while I'm gone. She'll need some help, if you know what I mean."

"Okay, what kind of help?"

"She's not as strong as she looks. We're soldiers and we know what it's about. She's sent me off too many times. I guess she thought that was over."

"So did I."

"Let's not get into that. I've got orders so there's nothing to talk about. I'll be gone a year. That's not long. We've been apart longer than that and everything turned out okay."

"If you say so."

They went to a gun store in Woodbridge and Paul spent over an hour admiring the firearms. He had become a certified expert and he knew the muzzle velocity and grain weight of everything in the store. He bought a Derringer two-shot handgun, a "mouse-gun" in the trade.

"I'll need this," he said. "You keep something like this in your hat. If you're captured and you're ordered to put your hand on your head, you can shot the guy who's in front."

"I thought this was a non-combat assignment."

"You never know. Be prepared. Isn't that what they say in the Boy Scouts. Don't tell your mother about this. There's no need to upset her."

His friends from ASA came to send him off, offering toasts and well wishes. Paul stood behind the bar in the basement of his home and smiled the smile of someone who was being sent into outer space. His expression was purely for the benefit of those toasting him. In his heart he had no desire to hear another shot fired in anger. He did not want to go to Vietnam. He did not want to fly on an airplane. He did not want to go to a place where people wanted to kill him. On his last night at home he had lain awake trying to make the faces of the ghosts go away. Before dawn, in his brief period of sleep, he had seen himself floating above the Earth crying to come down.

Two weeks later he was at Phu Bai as G2 NCO. G2 is tactical intelligence. He would be running intelligence to a Marine unit nearby and briefing them on what the Army had learned about the enemy in the past twenty-four to forty-eight hours. He was assigned a driver and a jeep, issued an M16 and combat gear, and told to keep his head down.

The ASA field station at Phu Bai was officially listed at the 8th Radio Research Unit. This was a vain attempt to explain the antenna field on the station. The real purpose of the station was to monitor Viet Cong, North Vietnamese, and Soviet radio traffic and to glean from that what the various units were doing. The Soviets were a primary supplier of weapons and materiel down the Ho Chi Min Trail and they used the same communications systems they employed in Europe, which made monitoring them easier. The Vietnamese, with a different sense of rhythm, were hard to copy on the Morse code frequencies until the ASA guys got used to the rhythm of the senders.

The Soviets also employed field teletype and other forms of modern communication. ASA direction-finding teams tracked the location of the Soviet and Vietnamese radio networks and analysts broke the codes that the Communists employed to decipher the messages that were being sent. It was the same game that was being played between Communist and Western units all over the globe.

Each side knew what the other was doing and part of the game was determining what was real and what was false. Analysts were the ones who kept score. They tracked the who-and-what of the other side and prepared reports. Paul's job was to brief the Marines on the best guesses of the analysts.

The truth was hard to come by in such an environment and the joke was that fifty per cent of what was in the reports was wrong, but no one knew which half. So Paul spent his days reading the reports, finding his driver, and heading for the Marines.

HHM164 was a medium helicopter unit that ferried Marines and supplies in that command area of Vietnam. They were known as the Knightriders. In 1966 the Knightriders flew CH-46 Sea Knight helicopters to support the Marine infantry units that were going after the North Vietnamese and Viet Cong units in the area.

American Intelligence had strong evidence that the North Vietnamese were using the demilitarized zone to send men and weapons into South Vietnam in clear violation of the international treaty that had split Vietnam a decade earlier. Marines patrolling near the DMZ had seen the NVA troops and one of North Vietnamese, a lieutenant, surrendered and said his forces were moving south. Intelligence put the number at fifteen-hundred.

The NVA units were large enough to be accompanied by Soviet advisers who were there to oversee some of the weapons they had provided. There was steady radio traffic that was being picked up at Phu Bai by the ASA interceptors and Paul was running the latest reports to the commanders of HHM164.

The Marines were ordered to drive the NVA back across the DMZ in July of 1966 in Operation Hastings. The operation would include a force of Marines and a force of South Vietnamese troops known as ARVN, for Army of the Republic of Vietnam. \

The need for intelligence was intense. Paul and his driver were busy on the roads and tracks that led to the Marine headquarters and the Viet Cong snipers in the area were active, taking shots at most of the jeeps and three-quarter ton trucks that were softer targets than the armored personnel carriers, APCs, and other heavier vehicles.

Each run was a shooting gallery. The snipers were hidden in thick vegetation and Paul could not spot them as he fired his M16 into the trees where the snipers were working. It was frustrating. He knew he wasn't hitting anything and that the advantage was with the VC, who had an open view of him and his driver on each run.

He got to know the First Sergeant of the headquarters company of HHM164, a beefy, pocked-faced man who ran a tight ship and passed the word that he would kick the ass of any Marine who crossed him. He, like Paul, was a combat veteran of earlier wars and the two men shared the occasional nip of bourbon and told war stories. Both men had doubts about the Vietnam War but kept those opinions to a small group.

"Goddam snipers are going to pick me off one of these days," Paul said. "I'm target practice for these guys. They could be throwing rocks and one of these days they'd hit me."

"What're you firing back with?" The First Sergeant asked.

"M16 but I can't see him so I'm just wasting ammo."

"That your only weapon?"

"I got a Derringer but it's even more worthless."

"Let me see."

Paul took the Derringer out of his hat and handed it to the Marine, who laughed.

"Why the hell do you keep it in your hat?"

"I thought it would come in handy if I got captured. Ain't much chance of that. But it's even more worthless against the sniper than the damned M16."

The Marine went to his rucksack and pulled out a black holster that held a Smith and Wesson State Police Model .357 magnum. "This son of a bitch will do the job."

"No it won't. It's a handgun and it won't hit anything at distance even if I could see him, which I can't."

"This ain't no ordinary .357. Check out these shells." The Marine offered a handful of rounds that had an odd shape at the tip of the brass. "Shot shells. I got 'em loaded with BBs. Fire off a couple of rounds and the son of a bitch will keep his head down. You won't kill him but he'll be pulling BBs out of his face while you drive off."

Paul thought it over. "What's the effective range on these babies?"

"The way I got 'em loaded, a hundred, hundred-fifty yards at least. Like I said, it won't be lethal but it will be effective. He'll wait for the next bus, if you get my drift."

"What do you want for it?"

"I'll take the Derringer even and all the ammo you got for it."

"I'll bring the ammo next time. If you don't mind, I'll leave the Derringer today and head out with that little shotgun you got there."

The sniper opened up on the trip back and Paul fired into the spot where he expected the sniper was hiding. It silenced him. The Smith and Wesson and its special loads were part of Paul's personal arsenal for the rest of his time in Vietnam and his daily gun battles were under control, more or less.

Every man has only so many gunfights in him. Only so many periods of combat. Only so much exposure to violence and death. For Paul, his limits were reached in Vietnam. It was hard to pinpoint the moment but was during the weeks when he was running intelligence to the Marines and expecting to be shot dead by a sniper on any one of the trips. It was as though his spirit had left his body. He drank when he could, which was often. He smoked constantly. He did not sleep. He read all night and worked all day. He lost weight. He lost his happiness. He looked like a man who had been emptied.

Finally, his tour ended and a C-130 took him from Phu Bai to Tan Son Nhut at Saigon, where he boarded a troop-filled passenger jet to the United States. He sat quietly, sipping from a flask, on the long trip to his home country. He did not speak to the other men and he did not eat. He had no expression on his face other than sadness. He looked into his future and saw nothing.

Chapter thirty-seven

Paul rode a train from San Francisco to Washington. He made a vow to himself that he would never fly again. He rode in a small, one person sleeper cabin and was drunk for the entire four day trip. He did not take off his uniform and he did not clean himself. The train pulled into Union Station in Washington where he would be greeted by Buddy and taken home.

Buddy walked into the waiting room expecting to see the man he had dropped off a year earlier, a smiling soldier, fit and ready to resume his life. It took him nearly half an hour to find his father. He walked through the crowds hoping for a shout or wave from a man standing with a duffel bag. There was no shout and no wave. Finally, after he had asked the information desk if the train had been delayed, he saw a man silently sitting on a bench, looking very small.

Buddy walked up to him and stopped. Paul looked up, then down at his shoes.

"Let's go home, Pop," Buddy said, picking up Paul's duffel bag.

The two men were silent as they drove across the 14th Street Bridge into Virginia. The sadness in the car sucked up all of the oxygen.

Buddy looked at his father as they drove down Interstate 95 to Woodbridge and the home where Marie was waiting. "How'd the Derringer work out?" He hoped to start a conversation.

"Traded it to a Marine for a .357," Paul replied.

"Traded up," Buddy said, hoping it would bring a smile to his father's face.

"It came with shot shells. I needed it for the snipers." Paul had no smile.

"How are you feeling?"

"I'm okay."

"You don't look okay."

"I'm okay. How's your mother?"

"She's anxious to see you. This has been hard on her."

"She's a good woman."

"You might want to think about pulling yourself together."

Paul turned to look at his son with an expression that contained a lifetime of hurt and fear. He said nothing.

Marie was waiting at the door when the car pulled into the driveway, a smile on her face. Buddy got out of the driver's side and went around to open his father's door. Paul sat still and stared straight ahead before he got out.

Buddy stood holding his father's duffel bag while his mother and father stared at each other. Both of them were crying. Marie pulled herself together and walked to Paul. She put her arm through his and walked him into the house. At that moment they were both casualties of war.

A neighbor had hung an American flag as a welcome home for Paul. Buddy looked at the flag and shook his head. How many families had paid a heavy price for it? How many good men were emptied of their will to go on? Do the people who live in this country have any idea?

A week later Paul reported for duty at Arlington Hall, more or less fit and ready. He was sober and clear-eyed. He was promoted to Sergeant Major and assigned as the top NCO in S2, strategic intelligence. His roommate from Phu Bai turned up at Arlington and the two of them formed a carpool to work. Life settled into a routine, but there was none of the happiness and exuberance that had marked their lives before Vietnam.

Paul never spoke of it. He went back to raising tomatoes and cantaloupes. He cleaned the .357 and the rest of his guns and inventoried his weapons and war trophies. He rarely smiled. His friends and family remarked that he was the saddest man they knew.

Buddy was married in early 1967 and Paul was drunk in the parking lot before the ceremony, passing a flask around to anyone nearby. It was a pattern that would follow him to the end of his life.

Marie, too, took on an air of sadness and resignation. All those years, all that worry, all the moves, and it came to this.

Paul put in his retirement papers in late 1967, sold the house, and he and Marie moved to Phoenix, Arizona to spend their remaining days in sunshine.

The 1980's

Chapter thirty-eight

"...dying is such a long tiresome business..."
Samuel Beckett

It took him twenty-two years to drink himself to death. Twenty-two years of sadness and regret. Marie's life had become unbearable and she often considered leaving him for her own sanity. He stayed up all night, reading and drinking, and slept most of the day, rising in a hangover and staggering into the bathroom to pull himself together.

His smoking had produced a cough that left him weak and searching for breath. His drinking had left him gaunt. He spent hours on the patio next to the pool in the back yard, trying to convince himself that it had all been worth it, but his ghosts came in these moments and he lost the thread of his quest for something resembling happiness.

He found a friend across the street, a swashbuckling former smuggler named Arlo who was making a living as an insurance adjuster, rock hound, and genuine Indian jewelry maker, although he didn't have a drop of Native American blood in him, but the tourists who bought his stuff didn't know that.

Arlo, too, was a man with a past and he had some good stories that kept Paul entertained for hours. He had smuggled God-knows-what all over Central and South America flying small planes and had crashed more than one. He had only a passing respect for written laws and even less for the customs of people whom he considered boring and irrelevant; those folks known as normal people. Arlo also had a taste for whiskey, something his sweet wife forbad. So Arlo's time in Paul's backyard offered something more than a story.

Paul had grandchildren in those years and when they came to visit he took them out into the desert and taught them how to shoot handguns, rifles and shotguns. He instructed them on gun safety and how to properly clean a weapon. He made them milk shakes in the evening and told them long, boring stories from the history books he consumed.

Marie went to church and prayed for him. She watched as the years took away her own hope for a happy retirement. He seemed to think only about drinking and guns. Their home was filled with the trophies military families accumulate; crystal from Germany, dolls from France, lamps from Japan. Art and antiques, photographs and memories of places far away.

At first, it was fun to have new friends over to show off the items of a lifetime of moves. Most people had never been very far from home and were impressed by the 17th Century Japanese mirror or the SS dagger that Paul had taken from a dead German officer.

Paul's life was long ago, it seemed, and he spent his days looking back, not forward. His mother was dying and he refused to talk to her. He had no desire to hear her voice one more time. To him, she had died long ago.

Charlie was dead, too. So was Herbert. Only his sister was alive and he cherished his calls to her but he could not bring himself to face his home in Dixie, even though Elizabeth's sweet Southern voice rang in his ears like a choral work. At times he just wanted to hear her speak, she could read the phone book as far as he was concerned.

Marie sank deeper into her own darkness, calling her family in Lowell to cry and announce that she couldn't take it anymore. She left Paul for a few weeks and visited Buddy and his wife, spending her evenings on the phone with Paul, crying and asking him to get help. But Paul was not a man to show his weakness to other men and he promised her that he could straighten out on his own. Marie went to a therapist and found a bit of happiness, but she could not live apart from Paul and she returned to Phoenix.

Paul was sober for a couple of weeks after she returned and then he had one drink, then two, and the old pattern came back to their lives. He spent his hours on the patio, staring into the pool, seeing the faces of the long dead.

He saw the face of the Soviet officer he had killed in a hallway and could not bring himself to apologize. Him or me, he thought. He saw the faces of the SS guards at Dachau and wished he could shoot them again. He saw the faces of Chinese soldiers at the Chosin

Reservoir and experience the fear all over again. So many of them coming at him. So many dead. So cold.

And, always, the face of the dead Marine who gave up his rifle so that Paul could live. How can such a debt be repaid? The Marine's weapon was even loaded and he had spare ammo. A gift like that cannot be accepted without payment, but how?

Buddy and his family came to visit once a year and in the early evening darkness around the pool Paul would whisper his secrets.

"They only thing they asked us after Dachau was why we didn't leave one guy to tell them what had happened," he said, looking into the darkness.

"I shot a German who was trying to blow up a fuel dump. We chased each other all afternoon."

"Son of a bitch who shot me gave me that Lugar."

"I never saw so many Chinks as in Korea. Damn. Didn't think I'd make it."

"Russians are some tough sons a bitches."

"Junior Gaston had the best mind for numbers I've ever seen. He could memorize pages of them and recite them back and not miss one."

"Steve Wargo was smart as hell. He fooled more than one Soviet border guard."

"You don't know what it's like to take a rifle from a dead man to survive."

"I respect the Germans but I hate Gooks. Gooks will string you up and skin you alive."

And so it went.

He had little contact with his Army friends. A few letters here and there but no calls and no visits.

He was still a young man but he had no desire to seek any kind of employment, despite offers from the CIA and the NSA. He was offered a job as an instructor at a local shooting range but turned it down. Marie tried to coax him into something resembling a life but he resisted, saying he didn't want to take a job from someone who needed it.

"You're not taking a job from anybody," she said. "No one else can do what you do."

He ignored her and drank away his nights in the company of his ghosts. His depression grew as his body shrank. He developed cancer of the mouth and had surgery that removed part of his tongue, making it difficult for him to speak. The cancer spread to other parts of his body and he went to the VA hospital for treatment, spending his time in the cantina with other old vets, smoking and telling war stories.

Marie's heart began to fail and she received a new valve to relieve her condition. She recovered from open heart surgery and got stronger.

He seemed to be failing and she made plans to move back to Lowell to live with her sister when the cancer took him. His doctors told her he didn't have long to live.

He was stronger than he looked. He kept rallying when doctors told Marie he was near the end. She was exhausted, emotionally and physically. On a clear and beautiful afternoon in April Marie went to her room to take a nap. As she slept, her heart gave out and her life was over. She was a spiritual, almost mystical person and in her last moments she saw her mother coming to take her.

Paul was asleep when she died. He woke up in the late afternoon and went to the bathroom to get himself together. He walked into the kitchen, expecting to find his wife preparing dinner. He called her name. He looked in the back yard to see if she was hanging clothes. He went into her room and found her peaceful, a soft look of happiness on her face. He sat next to her and called her name. Again. He touched her face and her neck and he fell apart. He cried out her name and he had trouble breathing. He had a moment when he could not stand being alive with her gone and he wanted to grab one of his guns and end it.

He had to call Buddy. He had to tell him that his mother was gone, he owed him that much. He dialed 911 and waited outside until they arrived and confirmed what he knew to be true. The only woman he had ever loved had left him.

He went into a period of heavy drinking that would have killed a man less used to the consumption of alcohol in large quantities. He barely got through her funeral and threw up near her grave as she was being lowered into the ground.

A few days later he begged Buddy to shoot him. A few days after that he was back in the VA hospital. On a sunny morning, he lay on his bed, out of his mind with pain and grief. A nurse gave him some morphine and left the room. He closed his eyes and drifted off. He felt at peace. He heard a sound like bees in the sunshine and saw a white light. Out of the light appeared a man in combat clothing. He came to Paul and held out his hand. Under the helmet was the face of the long-dead Marine. He was smiling and holding out his rifle. Paul reached out and took the weapon. He followed the Marine into the light.

Author's note:

This is a novel. That means that much of it is made up. In this case, scenes, characters and dialogue.

What does it mean when an author states that a novel is "based on real events?" In this case, this is the story of my father, Command Sergeant Major Lawrence C. Matthews. The bones of this story are real. I heard the tales all my life. The childhood in poverty in rural Alabama, riding the rails at a teenager, the ranch work and Tony the Wonder Horse. The gun frozen to his hand in Montana. In his version of his time in Oregon, he was the "assistant manager" of a hotel. His sister, my aunt, laughed at that and said, "It wasn't a hotel. It was a whorehouse and he was the bouncer."

The section about World War Two was taken directly from the 304th's official history and his letters to my mother, along with the few stories he told about it.

The section regarding the Korean War came from his letters and historical sources.

The letters quoted in the story are taken directly from his letters to my mother.

The section about spying in Europe in the 1950s came from his stories and my recollections of the time we spent in Germany. I actually fired the cane that was a shotgun and the men he worked with, the extraordinarily gifted ones, were our family friends. I was a decoy on our "fishing" trips during which he and a companion were heavily armed while we fished and they observed the border with East Germany.

The Vietnam section was also from his stories and my own experience with the Army Security Agency.

And, finally and sadly, the last years of his life were lived by us all.

This book is about his story but I would be remiss if I did not point out that my mother, Irene Marie Matthews, is as much the hero of this story as he is. She is a symbol of all that Army wives, and their sisters with the other services, endure and sacrifice as their spouses give their working lives to the military. She spent many years in fear and despair that he would not come home.

Finally, this story is a testimonial to courage and strength of a generation of Americans who suffered through grinding poverty and the Depression, and went on to save the world. They gave us far more than we are giving to our children and grandchildren.

Their sacrifice came at a price. We should all hold it dear.

The man in this photograph is a combat veteran of World War Two and also Korea. The photo was taken in Frankfurt, Germany in the mid 1950s, when he was a field spy for U.S. Military Intelligence. His job was to go behind the Iron Curtain to obtain information about the Soviet military units that were a constant threat to Western Europe at the height of the Cold War. He is wearing custom-tailored clothing that hides the weapons he is carrying: a P38 Walther, a small "mousegun," brass knuckles, a blackjack, and a British Commando knife. Not seen in the photo is a cane with an ornate handle. The "cane" was, in reality, a .20 gauge shotgun. The man was one of the unsung and unheralded men who risked their lives on dangerous missions to protect the freedom of Western Europe and, indeed, America itself. This man is subject of this story. He is my father.

Made in the USA
Lexington, KY
15 March 2014